Preaching Through the Bible

Exodus 1–20

Michael Eaton

Sovereign World

Sovereign World Ltd
PO Box 777
Tonbridge
Kent TN11 0ZS
England

ISBN 1 85240 311 X

The publishers aim to produce books which will help to extend and
build up the Kingdom of God. We do not necessarily agree with every
view expressed by the author, or with every interpretation of Scripture
expressed. We expect each reader to make his/her judgement in the
light of their own understanding of God's Word and in an attitude of
Christian love and fellowship.

Typeset by CRB Associates, Reepham, Norfolk.
Printed in the United States of America.

By the same author:

Genesis 1–11 (Preaching Through the Bible) – Sovereign World

Genesis 12–23 (Preaching Through the Bible) – Sovereign World

Genesis 24–50 (Preaching Through the Bible) – Sovereign World

Applying God's Law (Exodus 19–24) – Paternoster

Joshua (Preaching Through the Bible) – Sovereign World

1 Samuel (Preaching Through the Bible) – Sovereign World

2 Samuel (Preaching Through the Bible) – Sovereign World

1 Kings (Preaching Through the Bible) – Sovereign World

Ecclesiastes (Tyndale Commentary) – IVP

Hosea (Focus on the Bible) – Christian Focus

Joel and Amos (Preaching Through the Bible) – Sovereign World

The Way That Leads to Life (Matthew 5–7) – Christian Focus

Mark (Preaching Through the Bible) – Sovereign World

Luke 1–11 (Preaching Through the Bible) – Sovereign World

Return to Glory (Romans 3:22–5:21) – Paternoster

Living Under Grace (Romans 6–7) – Paternoster

1 Corinthians 1–9 (Preaching Through the Bible) – Sovereign World

1, 2 Thessalonians (Preaching Through the Bible) – Sovereign World

2 Timothy (Preaching Through the Bible) – Sovereign World

1 Peter (Preaching Through the Bible) – Sovereign World

1, 2, 3 John (Focus on the Bible) – Christian Focus

Living A Godly Life (Theology for Beginners) – Paternoster

Enjoying God's Worldwide Church (Theology for Beginners) – Paternoster

No Condemnation – IVCP (USA)

Experiencing God (Theology for Beginners) – Paternoster

General Preface

There is need of a series of biblical expositions which are especially appropriate for English-speaking people throughout the world. Such expositions need to be laid out in such a way that they will be useful to those who like to have their material or (if they are preachers), to put across their material in clear points. They need to avoid difficult vocabulary and advanced grammatical structures. They need to avoid European or North American illustrations. The *Preaching Through the Bible* series seeks to meet such a need. Although intended for an international audience I have no doubt that their simplicity will be of interest to many first-language speakers of English as well.

These expositions are based upon the Hebrew and Greek texts. The New American Standard Version and the New International Version of the Bible are recommended to the reader but at times the expositor will simply translate the Hebrew or Greek himself.

It is not our purpose to deal with minute exegetical detail, although the commentator has to do work of this nature as part of his preliminary preparation. But just as a housewife likes to serve a good meal rather than display her pots and pans, so we are concerned with the 'good meal' of Scripture, rather than the 'pots and pans' of dictionaries, disputed interpretations and the like. Only occasionally will such matters have to be discussed. Similarly matters of 'introduction' do not receive detailed discussion, but only as much as is necessary for the exposition to be clear. On occasions a simple outline of some 'introductory' matters will be included, perhaps in an appendix, but the first chapter of each exposition gets into the message of Scripture as speedily as possible.

I ought to emphasise that simplicity of style is not simplicity of content. Although on the surface written simply, these expositions aim at a high level of scholarship, and attempt to put the theological and practical message of each book of the Bible in a clear and down-to-earth manner. Simplicity of style is not simplicity of content. God's Word needs to be expounded with thoroughness, but the language needs to remain easy and accessible. Some progress in this direction is attempted in these expositions.

Contents

Contents

Author's Preface

I preached through Exodus in fifty-five broadcasts for Trans-World Radio some years ago. These chapters are the by-product of my work at that time, with revisions in 1996 when various fellowships in South Africa heard me preaching on 'The Call of God', in the form of expositions from the life of Moses. My friends in the lunchtime meetings of Chrisco Fellowship in Nairobi heard similar expositions shortly after. Also I have done more work on the Mosaic law, and these more recent expositions have, I hope, brought clarifications in what I preach. *Applying God's Law* (Exodus 19–24), published by Paternoster, gives a fuller exposition of the Ten Commandments and the surrounding chapters.

As always, I am grateful to Jenny, to Tina Gysling, my daughter, who worked through my material some years ago; to my son Calvin who lives in Nairobi and as a wise son often makes his father glad. And to Chris Mungeam and Tim Pettingale who give me steady encouragement – many thanks to you all.

Michael Eaton

Chapter 1

God's Faithfulness Amidst Change
(Exodus 1:1–22)

At the point where 'Exodus' begins Israel are in a situation of great difficulty. They had fallen into slavery and oppression in Egypt. The book of Genesis has told us the story of how men and women were created in God's image, but then fell into sin and darkness (Genesis 1–11). The later chapters of Genesis have told us of a promise of salvation that is to come through a 'seed of Abraham'. In Abraham, Isaac, Jacob and Joseph we have seen some models of faith and patience. Readers of Genesis should know by now that salvation is by grace and through faith. Before any legislation is given on Mount Sinai we are to know that salvation is by trusting God's promise. Abraham believed God and that was reckoned to him as righteousness (see Genesis 15:6). Yet Abraham was also told that there would come a time when his people would fall into slavery and would be ill-treated in a foreign land (Genesis 15:13). God would then liberate His people in a great and mighty deliverance.

Exodus to Numbers tell the story of the creation of Israel and its establishment as the people of God. In Exodus 1:1–15:21 we have the story of how the people of God came to be in need of deliverance by the blood of a lamb. The people were experiencing persecution and slavery (ch. 1). God prepared a deliverer, Moses (2:1–4:31). After an initial period of conflict with Pharaoh (5:1–7:7) there came a time when Pharaoh was confronted by nine powerful judgements from God (7:8–10:29), but it was a tenth judgement, the battle over the 'firstborn son', that led to the redemption of Israel by the blood of a lamb

(11:1–14:31). They march out of Egypt singing a song of triumph (15:1–21).

The rest of Exodus tells the story of the establishment of the people of God. They journey to Sinai (15:22–17:7), facing two different reactions to their redemption (17:8–18:27). Then they arrive at Sinai and the 'books of the law' record no further travelling until Numbers 10:11. The whole of Exodus 19:1 to Numbers 10:10 finds its setting at Mount Sinai. Our concern for the moment is with Exodus 1–20.

The story begins with 'salvation by the blood of a lamb'. It is a story which is relevant for the Christian for it gives us a sample of the way in which God works, and a preview of His altogether greater deliverance from sin and judgement 'through the blood of a lamb'. Jesus is the lamb of God.

All the principles of our salvation are to be found in the Old Testament. As we read Exodus we are not only reading about historical events – although the 'Exodus' was certainly historical. We are also reading of God and of the way in which He saves. At a higher level His way of salvation is still the same today. The human race is in bondage. No one can escape the power of sin. God prepares a deliverer, Jesus. Through the blood of God's lamb, there is escape from our sinfulness and bondage and we become pilgrims travelling to a promised land.

Exodus 1:1–5 begins by listing the seventy ancestors of the nation of Israel (the sixty-eight of Genesis 48:8–26 plus Jacob himself plus Joseph and two sons).[1] The whole people of God are involved in this event, and Exodus 1:1–5 emphasises the fact by listing the whole nation of Israel.

1. **The people of God go through a time of many changes and great difficulty**. The change came quite suddenly. A new situation was abruptly thrust upon them. None of us like change. We like to be in a routine that is safe and secure and goes on for ever. But God has a habit of allowing change to come in our lives and in the story of our nation. It makes us realise we are dependent on God. They had been progressing well and were growing in numbers (1:6–7). Their situation might have stayed that way indefinitely if God had not brought about a change. Often a time of change is a time of challenge

when we discover God's faithfulness in a new way. But when there are things happening that force change we must realise that God is giving us new opportunities and His kingdom is about to go forward in some way.

There came a new king that did not know Joseph (1:8). He does not like this ever-increasing number of Israelites in his country (1:9–10) and soon persecution and oppression start for God's people. Joseph their leader is no longer with them. They go through a time when they are not recognized as having any importance. It is always difficult to be less important than before in a society. Then they face fierce persecution. It comes in stages. (i) First, there is harsh treatment (1:11–14). (ii) Then there is secret persecution (1:15–20). Pharaoh does not say much publicly but there is a quiet campaign to exterminate the people by allowing only girls to live. If the programme had continued, soon there would be no men and the people would die out. (iii) When this does not work there is open persecution. Pharaoh issues a decree. *'Every boy that is born you must throw into the Nile'* (1:22).

Why does God allow such things to happen? Because unchanging progress makes us spiritually careless. We need changes in our lives to shake us up and drive us to seek God. Israel would not have been calling on God (2:23) if their life had continued to be a life of ease and privilege. The new events in the nation drive them to pray as never before (see 2:23).

2. **God is using oppression to prepare them for the future**. Despite what was happening to them God was with them. God gave them some bold and courageous women to help them. The midwives 'feared God' (1:17). God can give us people who favour us.

God prospered them numerically. They had been growing in numbers before (1:7); now they continued to grow in numbers despite all that Pharaoh was doing (1:20). Oppression could not crush them. God is able to preserve His people.

If we are going through a time of change or distress we can count it a matter of joy. We may not be enjoying precisely what is happening but if we let God work we shall discover He is moving us a stage further on in blessing and in His purpose.

God can work in our circumstances to shape our character and prepare our future. He does it with individuals; He can do it with His entire church. Every one of the sons of Israel are involved in what is happening (1:1–5). God was preparing His entire people for some dramatic forward steps in their history. He had told them what would happen centuries before (Genesis 15:13–14); now He is superintending what He predicted. Soon they will see great things happening. They will be redeemed by God's mighty stretched out arm and taken towards a new promised land.

Note

[1] The ancient Greek translation has 'seventy-five' here and in Genesis 46:27 and was followed by Stephen in Acts 7:14. Various reasons might be given for the change of figure. (i) In Genesis 48:8–26 there are sixty-six names. The Greek version added in verse 27 mention of nine sons of Joseph. (ii) In addition to the sixty-six, there was Jacob himself, Joseph and his two well-known sons, plus seven grandchildren mentioned in 1 Chronicles 7:14–15. 'Seventy-five' (rather than seventy-seven) might be a rough round figure. (iii) Stephen was adapting himself to the common tradition without bothering about pedantic accuracy. Scripture is accurate in recording what he said!

Chapter 2

The Faith of Moses' Parents
(Exodus 2:1–10)

God was taking note of the suffering of His people, and He had a saviour in mind, Moses. Yet as Jesus, at the time of his birth, was the object of Herod's hatred (Matthew 2:1–23), so Moses was in danger from his earliest days. But by faith Moses' parents rescued him.

1. **Their faith was stimulated by something natural**. When Moses' mother gave birth to her son he was a handsome child, and that prompted her to look for a way to rescue him. She was prompted by **natural** feelings. It was entirely a natural thing for a mother to want to protect a good-looking new-born son. Sometimes our faith shows itself along **natural** channels. Faith is a supernatural thing always, but it can flow along the channels of human desires. Sometimes what we want to do for God is the very thing God wants us to do for Him.

2. **Their faith delivered them from fear**. Pharaoh was a powerful ruler yet Moses' parents had the courage to defy the king. 'They were not afraid of the king's edict' (Hebrews 11:23). Faith and fear are opposites. Faith excludes fear; fear excludes faith. Faith shows itself by a refusal to panic. Moses' parents were able to stay calm in a crisis because they trusted God and were not afraid of the king.

3. **Their faith showed itself in the form of instinct**. Sometimes we have a kind of instinct about what we ought to do. Generally faith is response to a clear 'word' from God, but at other times there is not exactly a clear word. Instead there is a sense of something we ought to do although we are not 100% sure about it. Moses' parents felt they at first ought to hide their

son. They were following what we might call spiritual instinct, but the Bible calls it 'faith' (Hebrews 11:23).

4. **Their faith had its limits**. For three months they felt confident about simply ignoring the decree of Pharaoh and keeping Moses at home, but when Moses began to get somewhat bigger they no longer had the faith to keep him and felt they should do something else. God took them so far along that direction but then their faith could go no further along those lines.

We are to do everything we have faith for, but we should act within the limits of our faith. We should do that for which we have assurance, but not that which will bring us into being full of doubts. We all have only a 'measure' of faith (Romans 12:6). If we try to go beyond it we shall find ourselves being 'double-minded, unstable in all or ways' (see James 1:5–8). Moses' parents had faith to hide Moses for three months but their faith did not take them any further in that direction.

5. **Their faith led them into action**. Faith on its own is useless to help other people or achieve anything for God. Moses' parents had faith but it was faith plus works. They believed in God, but their belief led them to take practical steps to protect their son. Their faith was not useless faith; it was active faith, working faith.

Saving faith is without works, but then saving faith has to become continuing faith. Continuing faith **does** have works in it. The parents of Moses felt they had to do something. They felt they should put their new-born son in a basket and place him in the river Nile. If we have faith in our heart it will lead us to see the challenges of God and then do something.

6. **Their faith led them into civil disobedience**. Generally a Christian should be obedient to governing authorities – but not when they are commanding the murder of baby boys! There is a time when it is right to refuse obedience to governing authorities. No secular leader has the authority to command murder. We do not have to obey governing authorities when they command us to do something sinful. We shall respect them at other points, but if they command something that is clearly wicked we must 'obey God rather than men' (see Acts 4:19;

5:29). We must not make this into an excuse for being rebellious towards governments all the time, but there might be times when we must refuse obedience. Here is a case of people refusing to obey a king out of regard for God and His ways. They have faith to believe God can rescue their child. And they have faith to defy the king. It is civil disobedience in faith.

Their faith leads them to put Moses into the river. In a sense they are obeying the king. Pharaoh said baby boys should be put in the river. They are putting him into the river. Pharaoh did not say you could not use a basket!

Then there is an amazing turn of events. The basket rests in the river. Pharaoh's daughter sees the boy and takes him for her own (2:3–6). Moses' sister was not far away and offered the services of a woman to nurse the baby (2:7). Moses' mother was instructed by Pharaoh's daughter to look after her own son, and got a salary from the palace for doing it! Pharaoh had wanted to kill baby Moses, but actually his daughter paid his mother a salary to look after him.

In every situation God has got a plan for us and for His kingdom. We follow what we sense is His guidance. He will honour us and we shall achieve something for His kingdom. Moses' parents had the joy of getting their son back, but they had also achieved something for God. This child that they had delivered from Pharaoh would one day deliver the whole people of Israel from Pharaoh.

Act up to the full measure of your faith, and you will end up doing something wonderful for Him and for His kingdom.

Chapter 3

Faith and Failure

(Exodus 2:11–22)

Faith has got many stages and many aspects to it. We may consider faith as saving faith, as diligent faith, as faith amidst training, as faith at the time of death – and so on. Basically faith is believing God, but there are many angles from which faith can be considered.

1. **Faith is seeing things the way God sees them**. Moses considers the Hebrews in Egypt. He himself is the adopted son of Pharaoh's daughter. He is living a leisurely upper-class life, but he knows that he was born from Hebrew parents. Most people in Egypt, when they thought about the Hebrews, thought of them as being a small tribe of foreigners who should be used as slaves. But Moses knows about the promises of God and he believes in these promises. Faith is seeing things the way God sees them. It is seeing God as a Saviour, seeing His willingness to save me, knowing with a gripping conviction that He will save me.

2. **Faith is a conviction that leads to a willingness to suffer**. Moses *'went out to his brothers'* (2:11). He left the life in Pharaoh's palace and began to identify with the Hebrews. He did so regardless of the cost. It did not matter to him that he was losing his privileges in the palace. He knew that the promises of God about the Hebrews were true and so chose to endure ill-treatment with the people of God rather than the luxuries of the palace.

3. **Faith is putting righteousness above profit and financial gain**. There was wealth for him in the palace, but Moses looked for 'greater riches than the treasures of Egypt'. His faith made

him know that the reward of God was worth having more than the treasures of Egypt.

4. **Faith is knowing now what everyone will know one day**. Moses believed that the future of the Hebrews was destined to be wonderful. Not many others believed that. Faith is seeing the way things will be before others see it. Faith is knowing, simply on the basis of what God has said, that things will turn out the way God has predicted. The Christian knows that Jesus is the King of kings. He knows that Jesus will come again to planet earth. One day everyone will know this, but the Christian knows it now. One day every knee will bow, but the Christian bows the knee now. Moses was 'looking for the reward' (Hebrews 11:26).

However although Moses was a man of faith he was not completely ready to be used by God in a great way. Moses' story is a story of faith but at first it is also a story of failure.

1. **Sometimes God uses an experience of failure in our lives**. At first Moses failed in getting God's will done. He sees an Egyptian beating a Hebrew (2:11). He thinks no one is watching and kills the Egyptian (2:12). Moses had a desire in his heart to rescue Israel from its slavery. That desire came from God but Moses' way of going about matters was not right. God did not instruct him to kill any Egyptian. And the time was not yet right. Moses did not yet have any clear call from God to be Israel's deliverer.

The next day Moses intervenes when two Hebrews are fighting (2:13) and one of them says *'Who made you a prince or a ruler over us?'* (2:14). Israel was rejecting Moses' leadership. When Moses discovers that his killing the Egyptian was known he was afraid. Acting without God's leading leads to bad mistakes and then it leads to fear. Moses is trying to do God's will without having the leading of God. Actually he will one day be the prince and ruler of Israel but he is acting prematurely.

Moses has to leave Egypt (2:15). He does so with faith but also with failure. He had deliberately identified with the people of God, the Hebrews, but the way he had done things had failed.

2. **God uses delay as a means of preparing us**. Moses runs to Midian. He is a born leader and an energetic man. When he sees

the daughters of the priest of Midian being badly treated (2:16–17) he rescues them and then helps them. It is precisely what he will do one day for Israel. He will rescue Israel from their oppressors. He will give them good laws from God to help the nation. Moses is a leader and a rescuer by his temperament. He was born to be a rescuer. He watched the Israelites (2:11) and stopped a fight (2:13). He helps these girls. It is part of what he is like as a human personality. Yet he is self-willed. He was doing these things in Egypt in a secretive, shameful way (2:12). He did not yet have any calling from God. Moses soon gets to meet the father of the girls at the well (2:18–20). Not long after he marries one of them (2:21) and settles down in Midian (2:22).

God is delaying before letting Moses do what he wants to do. (i) Moses must learn to do things in God's way and at God's time. His desire to rescue Israel is truly from God, yet he is not yet ready. He must learn to avoid self-confidence. (ii) He must learn to be in God's timing. (iii) He must learn through hardship. He has been living in a palace. It has been a life of luxury and ease. That is not a good preparation for the work of God. Now he is in Midian where he is a *'temporary resident in a foreign land'* (2:22). He lives in a desert and will stay there for years. (iv) He needed humbling. Moses became a very meek person but he was not born a meek person. He needed training. He needed to have his patience stretched. He needed to go through some suffering. Then he would be ready and God would use him.

Chapter 4

Called to Serve God

(Exodus 2:23–4:13)

God was taking note of Israel's plight. The Pharaoh, the father of the Egyptian princess who adopted Moses, died. It did not lead to any change in the situation for Israel (2:23), but God was taking note of their plight and He was preparing a rescuer (2:24–25).

Moses had been prepared. Now there comes the greatest aspect of his preparation: a vision of the glory of God.

1. **Moses' call comes amidst faithfulness in small things**. Moses was continuing in his work as a shepherd and took his sheep to the west side of the desert (3:1). Then, not far away from where he was working 'the angel of Yahweh' appeared to him (3:2a). This is like the vision of God that had been experienced by Abraham many years before (Genesis 12:7). It is something physically visible. The angel represents God Himself. But the actual 'stuff' which is appearing is indeed an angel. 'He makes his angels into winds; he makes his servants into flames of fire' (Hebrews 1:7). The appearance is a **partial** appearance of the glory of God, represented by an angel.

2. **Moses' call begins with an experience of the holiness of God**. The first ingredient in any call from God is an experience of God. It will not necessarily be exactly the same almost-unique experience that Moses had, but it is something comparable. The person called to ministry must know God. He must know that God has spoken to him. He must be gripped with the conviction by the Spirit, and by other ways of guidance, that God is indeed calling him into this particular work for Him. Every Christian has gifts which are to be used for God's

kingdom. Every Christian has some kind of calling. And God is willing to speak to us to reveal what that calling is.

The manifestation of God to Moses was one of blazing fire which did not need to consume anything in order to shine. Most fires need some kind of fuel, but this is a fire which does not need to draw upon fuel outside of itself.

The fire spoke of God's holiness. Fire is that which consumes anything rubbishy, anything unsubstantial. It is that which illuminates sin and strikes out at it to destroy it.

Moses reacts with curiosity and begins to stroll towards the bush which is burning but not burning. It strikes him as strange as he sees it in the distance (3:2b) and he begins to walk up to it with an enquiring mind and a desire to investigate (3:3). As he approaches his casual attitude is rebuked. *'Take off your sandals, for the place on which you are standing is holy ground'* (3:4–5). Then God reveals Himself and Moses responds with awe, amazement and humility (3:6).

3. **Moses' call began with an appeal to his compassion.** God calls Moses to go to Egypt as the rescuer of God's people. He puts the need before Moses. A call to ministry normally involves being burdened with a sense of the needs of others. God speaks to Moses about the sufferings of His people (3:7), and about His desire to rescue them (3:8), and His desire to overcome their oppressor (3:9).

Then he summons Moses to be the one that He will use. *'So now, go. I am sending you...'* (3:10). But now Moses does not want go! There had been a time, many years previously, when he had appointed himself as the rescuer of Israel. At that time he had been acting in self-will. But now God calls him to do the very thing he had wanted to do, only now he does not want to do it!

Moses has five objections:

i. He thinks he is inadequate. *'Who am I that I should go...?'* (3:11)

ii. He believes that he does not know enough. *'Suppose I go ... and they ask me "What does his name mean?" What shall I tell them?'* (3:13).

iii. He fears that he will be ineffective. *'What if they do not believe me or listen to me...?'* (4:1).

iv. He thinks he lacks the appropriate gifts. *'O Yahweh I have never been good at speaking . . . '* (4:10).

v. He would prefer that someone else should do the work instead. *'O Yahweh, please send someone else . . . '* (4:13).

This is a strange thing. When Moses wanted to do the work God was not sending him. Now God is sending him Moses does not want to do the work. The truth is that we often want to do God's work for the wrong reasons. Moses was naturally fitted to be a rescuer of Israel. He knew all about Egypt. He had grown up in the palace. He was a strong and capable man. Surely, one might think, this is the ideal man to be God's leader. Maybe. But God does not want people who are 'naturally' the right leader. The ability is not a call.

To some extent Moses had the right heart. He was a man of compassion. He felt for the people of Israel and wanted to identify with them and do something to get them out of their plight. On the other hand when a person truly sees what is involved in a call from God it is rather terrifying. God is a holy God. He is sending people on holy business. It is a very serious thing to be a representative of God. Who is worthy of it? When we truly see what is involved in serving God as His spokesman, as His worker, the minister of His word, we shrink from it and feel it to be totally above us.

A man who has never feared to represent God is probably not truly called of God. A person who shrinks in fear at least has the right attitude. He at least knows that he is starting on something which is high and holy. He might want to run from his call. But the voice of God keeps on coming, and God does not take no for an answer.

Chapter 5

God's Answers

(Exodus 3:11–22)

Moses made five protests when God called him to Egypt, but God simply kept calling him despite all of his difficulties and objections. This is what a call from God is like. Those who are truly called by God are often quite reluctant to obey God, but God will not let them go and puts pressure on them to obey what He is challenging them to do.

1. **God answers Moses' feeling of inadequacy** (3:11–12). Moses thinks he is inadequate for the task. 'Who am I that I should go . . . ?' (3:11). So God answers him.

God says *'I will be with you'* (3:12a). It is as if God is saying: 'But Moses, I never said you were adequate and I am not asking you to be adequate. Your strength is going to come from me. When you go to Egypt I shall be with you. I will show you what to do, and will be with you as you do it'.

Then God promises Moses a sign: *'And this will be the sign to you that it is I who have sent you. When you have brought the people out you will worship God on this mountain'* (3:12b). It is a somewhat surprising sign since Moses will not get it until he has obeyed God! Moses might want to say 'But I want a sign now, not one that I get after I have done everything you are telling me'. But God's signs are sometimes like that. This is not a sign before Moses obeys; it is a sign he will get from God after he obeys. We often would like some sign before we obey God. But God tends to give us confirming signs as and when we obey Him, or maybe after we have obeyed Him. To those who obey God gives confirmations.

2. **God answers Moses' conviction that he does not know enough** (3:13–22). Moses is troubled by his ignorance of God's

23

name. For a long time people had used the name 'Yahweh'. It is
an extremely archaic word. It is linked with the verb 'to be' and
almost certainly means 'HE IS'. It is generally translated LORD
(with capital 'L', capital 'O', capital 'R' and capital 'D').
Whenever we find LORD in our English Old Testaments it is
the translation of the very name of God, Yahweh (or as it
is sometimes spelt 'Jehovah').

The people of God had the idea that there was something
mysterious about this name – and they were right. Jacob had
asked God the meaning of His name (Genesis 32:29) but at that
time God had given no answer. Now that the people are about
to be redeemed by the blood of a lamb, the time is right for
God to reveal the deepest meaning of who and what 'HE IS'.

First God says 'I AM THAT I AM'. This is the fullest form
of the name of God. God is 'I AM THAT I AM'. Then God
says: *'This is what you are to say ... "I AM" has sent me to you'*
(3:14). We notice that the name has been shortened. First it was
I AM THAT I AM. Now it is shorter: I AM. Then God says:
Say to the Israelites, 'YAHWEH ... has sent me.' This is a
further shortening of the name. First it was I AM THAT I
AM; then it was I AM. Now it is YAHWEH (or 'HE IS').

This is the vital point. **Yahweh is the name 'I AM THAT I
AM' shortened to one word**. It is as though God says to Moses,
'Watch and see what is about to happen right now and that is
exactly what I am and what my name means'. God's name 'I
AM' is not about some philosophically abstract quality in God.
It is not about His absolute being or about His necessary
existence. Those are Greek philosophical ideas. When Philo,
the first century Jewish contemporary of Jesus and of Paul, said
'he speaks of the necessity of himself, saying I AM THAT I
AM', he was influenced by Greek philosophical ideas. Many
Christians have also read ideas of 'eternity' or 'absoluteness'
into God's name. But these 'philosophical' approaches miss the
point. What we have here is a reference not to philosophy but
to history! God says 'I AM THAT I AM' in what is about to
happen right now!

In one sentence: **God's name refers to His redeeming His
people by the blood of a lamb**. What God was about to do would

be a revelation of His name and His nature. 'Yahweh' means: the God of the Exodus, the God who takes a people for Himself, rescuing them from bondage, bringing them into newness of life **by means of the blood of a lamb**.

This is God's 'memorial name' (3:15), the name by which He is to be remembered for ever. Even in heaven Jesus will be 'the lamb as it had been slain'. God's memorial name will continue for ever, through the blood of Jesus.

There is another answer to Moses' anxiety about knowledge. He will discover that God is a God who can give direct and amazing knowledge to His servants. As Moses goes down to Egypt he will have knowledge enough to do everything that God wants him to do. Moses goes to Egypt with full knowledge of what God will do. He knows the elders will receive him (3:16–18a). He knows that he must ask for a period of leave for the Israelites (3:18b) and he knows that Pharaoh will refuse (3:19). He knows that God will work wonders (3:20) and then that the people will be released altogether (3:21). He knows that when they are released they will be abundantly provided for (3:22).

Moses had complained about not knowing enough. The truth is God can give us detailed and exact guidance. When Moses knows about the blood of the lamb and when He knows what God will do – He knows enough!

Chapter 6

The Promise of Effectiveness

(Exodus 4:1–31)

God continues to answer all of Moses' questions.

3. **God answers Moses' fear that he will be ineffective** (4:1–9). 'What if they do not believe me or listen to me...?' he asks (4:1). God answers him with the promise of three miracles, all of which are symbolic.

The stick which becomes a snake. First God says, 'What is that in your hand?' 'A staff', Moses replies (4:2). 'Throw it on the ground', says God, and as Moses does so it turns into a writhing dangerous snake (4:2–3).

It is God's way of saying 'Take yourself as you are, take the situation as it is, take what you have within your grasp. You may feel yourself to be nothing but a dead piece of wood, but throw yourself down before me and I will turn you into something that Pharaoh will fear!'

Then God tells Moses to reach out for the snake and 'take it by the tail' (4:4). Moses obeys God and it turns back into a harmless stick again. The tail is not the best part of a snake to grasp. If dangerous, it should be killed by crushing its head! It is God's way of saying 'Grasp boldly after the most dangerous things and I will make them harmless to you'. This sign is not for Moses only but for the people of Israel. When Moses works these signs in Egypt it will be a confirmation of Moses' claims (4:5), but it will also be a message about how God can make what is harmless into something dangerous, and can make what is dangerous into something harmless.

The hand that becomes leprous. Then God says 'Put your hand inside your cloak'. Moses does so and when he takes it out his hand is full of leprosy (4:6). It is as if God is saying: 'Your sense of weakness and fear' comes because you feel leprosy within yourself. Moses puts his hand on his heart, so to speak, and finds leprosy within. Then he puts the leprous hand back in his cloak and when he takes it out it is clean and restored (4:7). God is saying 'I am able to deal with the leprosy within', 'I am able to cleanse you within'. This too is to be a sign for the people of Israel (4:8).

The water that becomes blood. God offers a third sign. Moses is to take water from the Nile and pour it out on the ground. It will turn into blood. The Nile was the source of all life and fertility for Egypt and was worshipped as a god. Moses' sign takes the life-giving water which was worshipped and it becomes blood, the symbol of death. It is God's way of saying 'Don't be afraid of Egypt. I am able to ridicule the gods of Egypt'.

4. **God answers Moses' fear that he lacks sufficient gifts of speech** (4:10–12). Moses thinks he lacks the appropriate gifts. 'O Yahweh I have never been good at speaking...' (4:10). God answers his difficulty. *'Who gave man his mouth? Who makes him deaf? ... Who gives him sight?'* (4:11–12). All gifts and capacities are given by God or withdrawn by God. If Moses needs gifts of speaking, if the people need the ability to hear, if Pharaoh's heart is to be allowed to remain hard – every ability of communication or receptivity is within God's control, to give or to withhold. Why is Moses speaking about lacking gifts of speech?

5. **God is angry at Moses' continued reluctance** (4:13–17). Moses pleads that someone else should be sent (4:13) and at this point God becomes angry. Moses loses part of his call! Part of the work that God was offering for Moses to do is now to be given to Aaron (4:14–17). However it must be noted this is God's responding to Moses in anger. It is possible to lose part of what God is calling us to do. At last Moses is willing to respond to God. He goes to Jethro and tells him what he plans to do (4:18).

It is worth noting that at this point Moses gets plenty of encouragement. His family is sympathetic. Jethro is happy for him to go (4:18). Moses sets out for Egypt and his wife and sons go with him (4:19–20). He discovers that the Pharaoh he feared has died (4:19). God gives him further instructions (4:21). Again he is given a full revelation of what will happen when he gets to Egypt (4:22–23).

However there is another lesson for him to learn. As he goes back to Egypt he almost died. God was about to kill Moses (4:24)! Why was this? It was because Moses had not bothered to circumcise his sons. God had told Abraham 'Every male ... shall be circumcised ... Any uncircumcised male ... will be cut off...' (Genesis 17:10, 14). Moses had married a Midianite woman and had neglected the circumcision of his son. It seemed a small thing, but how can Moses be the servant of God if he will not keep the sign of God's covenant to Abraham? It is God's covenant to Abraham which is about to be fulfilled. How can part of it be ignored? Zipporah takes action and circumcises her son (4:25), associating Moses with what she has done (4:26). Then Moses recovers (4:26).

Moses is having to learn faithfulness. God wanted an obedient servant. Even Moses came under God's fatherly anger. Later Moses would build the tabernacle for God, and God would want him to be faithful in every detail. Moses is learning faithfulness in detail even now.

Then he is given another encouragement. Aaron meets him (4:27–28). They go to Israel and the elders of the people are convinced about what they say (4:29–31). Moses had had so many fears, but as he moves forward in obedience to God, all of his fears prove to be groundless. This is the way it is when we are in God's will. He stays with us. He gives us the knowledge and the guidance that we need. He enables us to be effective for Him, giving us the gifts that we need. He works both in leaders and in followers. He is utterly faithful.

Chapter 7

Attention to Details
(Exodus 5:1–6:13)

Moses became famous for faithfulness and for meekness. At one stage of his life God gave him a detailed plan for the building of the tabernacle and Moses did everything *'just as Yahweh commanded him'* (Exodus 40:16). 'Moses was faithful in all God's house' (Hebrews 3:2). However Moses was not always minutely and exactly obedient to God. Moses later gained a reputation for meekness (see Numbers 12:3), but he had not always been that way!

1. **Detailed faithfulness was something Moses had to learn**. We have seen that he had to learn to be faithful in the matter of the circumcision of his son. Also when Moses first went to Pharaoh he was not at first minutely faithful. According to Exodus 3:18 Moses was told (i) to take elders with him when he went to Pharaoh (3:18). (ii) He was to explain who 'Yahweh' was and should speak of 'Yahweh, the God of the Hebrews'. (iii) They were to be polite: '**Please** let us take a three-day journey...' (the Hebrew of this phrase is polite). (iv) They were to ask only for a temporary release for a three-day journey, to offer sacrifices to Yahweh.

But Moses was quite careless in the way he obeyed these instructions. He takes Aaron and they go to Pharaoh. We notice (i) Moses did not take the elders. Moses and Aaron went alone. (ii) The polite language of Exodus 3:18 was not followed. Without any courtesy and with no explanations they speak demandingly and abruptly. *'Thus says Yahweh, God of Israel: "Let my people go..."'* (5:1). (iii) Moses used the term 'Yahweh, God of Israel' which did not make sense to Pharaoh who did not know the term 'Yahweh' or the term 'Israel'.

(iv) Moses gave the impression that he was asking for total release – although God had said this would only come eventually after His forceful judgements upon the land.

2. **Moses' lack of attention to detail brought added burdens upon the Israelites**. Pharaoh refused to let Israel go (5:2). God had said this would happen but Pharaoh was more hostile than God had said. Moses tried to explain (5:3), as he should have done from the very beginning. He became more accurate in his request (5:3). But it was too late. An arrogant demand has produced an arrogant response. Pharaoh intensifies the oppression of Israel (5:4–9). When the people put a petition before Pharaoh they discover Moses' visit to Pharaoh is the cause of their added burdens (5:10–19). Then they blame Moses and Aaron for their troubles (5:20–21).

God had told Moses what would happen (see 3:16–22) but there was no mention of increased suffering for the Israelites and God had said nothing about the Israelite leaders criticising Moses. Moses' tactlessness as he spoke to Pharaoh brought added suffering which was no part of God's original plan.

3. **Moses' mistakes drive him back to God**. Moses' failing to attend to the manner with which he was to approach Pharaoh has got him into trouble, but he knows what to do with his mistake. *'Then Moses returned to Yahweh . . .'* (5:22). He puts all his questions and complaints to God (5:22–23). That is the best thing to do when we go wrong and disaster comes upon us. We take it to God. When a promise seems not to be fulfilled ('You have not delivered this people . . . !') we turn the promise into prayer.

4. **God simply encourages Moses with renewed promises**. God does not answer Moses' question ('Why have you brought harm . . . ?'). Moses himself will have to give more thought to his lack of attention to detailed obedience, and his lack of meekness. All that God does is give Moses fresh encouragement.

He assures Moses that God's plan is about to go forward. God is about to act more forcefully, and 'under compulsion' Pharaoh will yield to God's wishes (6:1). He reminds Moses that He is about to reveal the meaning of His name, Yahweh (6:2–3). God is about to give meaning to the name 'Yahweh'.

Previously, God had revealed Himself mainly as 'El Shaddai' – the God who has mighty power to rescue the helpless. Now He is about to give content and definition to the name 'Yahweh'. The name was known before but its full significance was not realised. Jacob had wanted to know God's name (Genesis 32:29) but God had not answered him. He lets Moses know that He is about to further establish the covenant-oath given to Abraham, Isaac and Jacob (6:4). God had given a 'covenant of generosity' to Abraham. The oath had been given (Genesis 22:16); it was absolutely certain that the promise to Abraham would be fulfilled. What was not quite certain was the timing. God lets Moses know that a new move is about to be made. God is taking a further step to fulfil His sworn promise to Abraham.

Moses must realise how much sympathy God has for the Hebrews (6:5) and must pass on a word of encouragement to them (6:6–8). Moses passes on the message but the Hebrews are too despondent to take it to heart (6:9). It is the first hint that although the Hebrews will be saved by faith (see Hebrews 11:29), their faith will be weak, despondent and sometimes rebellious. Moses is learning lessons of faithfulness. He is learning to be faithful himself, despite the weakness of his people and the greatness of any discouragements that will come to him.

5. **Moses is re-commissioned**. Despite the sufferings that have come because of Moses' imprecise obedience, God begins again with Moses. He sends Moses back to speak to Pharaoh (6:10–11). Moses is doubtful (6:12), but Aaron will go with him and the command is emphatic. They must do as God is saying (6:13). Moses' unsteady response to God's call makes no difference to God. God does not change His mind about us because of our unsteadiness. The call of God in Moses' life continues.

Chapter 8

The Family Line of Levi
(Exodus 6:14–7:7)

God had told Moses that Pharaoh would refuse to allow the Hebrews to go on a three-day journey to worship Him, but then as a result of 'an outstretched arm and ... great judgements' (6:6) Pharaoh would be compelled not only to let them go, but would send them away totally and permanently.

Moses will return to Pharaoh and work the signs of his power, as confirmations of his status as a servant of God (7:8–13). Then ten powerful punishments will come upon Pharaoh (7:14–11:10), each of them putting great pressure on him to release the people of Israel. In the tenth judgement, and by means of the blood of the lamb, the people will be released.

At this point the story-teller turns aside for the moment to relate the genealogy of Moses. It is his way of saying 'This is the precise person who was used at this moment of history to bring a great turning-point in the history of the nation'.

1. **The message of the Bible is rooted in historical facts**. Many religions are simply theories or ideas but the gospel of our Lord Jesus Christ is not like that. It does not begin in the theories of men and women; it begins with the things that God has done in history. God is not a theory; He is not a philosophical idea; He is not a theology. God is the living God. He acts. He has intervened in history and He is willing to intervene in our own lives. The writer inserts a genealogy at this point because he wants us to know exactly who Moses and Aaron were in the historical account of Israel. These events in the book of Exodus are factual; Moses and Aaron were real people, and real events took place in their lives.

32

The Family Line of Levi

The narrator begins with the three oldest sons of Jacob, starting with the firstborn son, Reuben. The narrator lists Reuben's sons (6:14), then Simeon's people (6:15), then those of Levi (6:16). Then he proceeds to list Levi's three grandsons, Gershon (6:17), Kohath (6:18) and Merari (6:19).

Aaron and Moses descended from Amram in the line of Kohath (6:20). Exodus 6:21–25 identifies some major figures in the tribe. The 'family tree' is as follows:

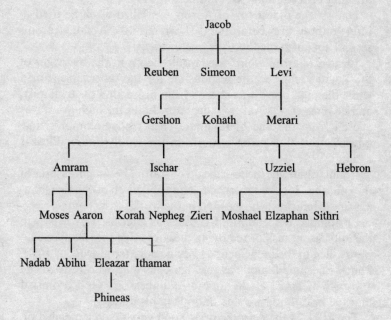

The tribe of Levi was divided into three section. There were the lines of Gershon, Kohath and Merari. Later on, Gershon's family carried the curtains and coverings from the tabernacle at the times when it was being moved. The Kohathites were another of the three divisions of the tribe. They had charge of the most vital pieces of furniture in the tabernacle. The Merarites looked after the boards and pillars of the tabernacle and other accessories to the tabernacle worship.

Amram was probably Aaron's ancestor, rather than his father in the strict sense; alternatively Amram the father of Aaron was named after an earlier Amram.

Uzziel, a Kohathite, is known through those of his descendants who brought up the ark to Jerusalem in the days of David (1 Chronicles 15:10).

Korah is known as the man who later would challenge Moses' authority and would be swallowed up by the earth opening beneath him (see Numbers 16–17).

Nadab, the oldest son of Aaron was killed when he tried to offer 'unholy fire' before God (Leviticus 10). Abihu, Aaron's second son, also died in the same incident.

Eleazar, Aaron's third son, would be given the oversight of the Levites and became responsible for the tabernacle. For a while the high priest was chosen from his section of the family, and he himself was Aaron's successor. Later the high priest was chosen from the line of Ithamar. Then from Solomon's time onwards the high priest came from the family-line of Eleazar again.

Ithamar himself, the fourth son of Aaron, became treasurer of the offerings for the tabernacle, and supervisor of the Gershonites and Merarites who assisted in the work of the temple.

Elzaphan a descendant of Uzziel was later used by Moses in the unpleasant task of removing the corpses of the relatives who were killed in the judgement of Leviticus 10 (see Leviticus 10:4). Phineas became famous as the righteous man who resisted the apostasy of Israel at the time of Numbers 25. God promised that the priesthood would continue in his family.

The work of the Aaronic priesthood very much depended on the tribe of Levi and on the three sections of his tribe that came from Gershon, Kohath and Merari. The information given here in (6:14–25) helps us to understand later regulations in the Mosaic law. But for the moment the genealogy mainly defines who Moses and Aaron are: 'It was this Moses and Aaron ... These are the ones...; it was this Moses and Aaron' (6:26–27).

2. **The message of the Bible is rooted in prediction**. Moses was told in advance what would happen. The story of redemption is a matter of prediction-and-fulfilment. Moses was fearful about

going to Pharaoh (6:28–30) but God provided Aaron as a speaker (7:1) and once again Moses was given detailed prior knowledge of what was about to happen (7:2–5).

3. **The message of the Bible has to be personally accepted**. God is giving a revelation. 'The Egyptians will know that I am Yahweh' (7:5). This does not mean that the Egyptians would experience God's salvation, but it means that they would be given enough knowledge to be able to respond to Him if they wished. God does enough to make us without excuse, even if we do not receive His word fully and totally.

Few of Pharaoh's people came to faith, but Moses and Aaron responded to God's call. The two men were obedient (7:6); Moses was eighty years old (7:7). Two-thirds of his life had passed but he was about to begin the greatest time of his life. God's Word requires responsiveness. When we respond to Him, the salvation of God is given to us and we find ourselves being used in His kingdom.

Chapter 9

Miracles True and False
(Exodus 7:6–13)

Moses and Aaron were obedient to God's instructions (7:6). It had taken time to get them to the point of obedience. Moses is eighty years old; Aaron is eighty-three (7:7). God may take a long time getting us to the point of willing obedience and readiness to do His will. Now at last Moses and Aaron have reached a great day in their lives. Three things have brought Moses especially to the point of obedience.

1. **He has been purged of all self-centred motives**. Many years before he had wanted to be the leader of Israel, but at that time he was rather self-confident and self-centred. He has now been cleansed of false motivation.

2. **He has been trained by suffering**. Suffering may be used to produce the best qualities in us. God brings us to the point where we are willing to be utterly obedient to God. Even Jesus learned obedience by suffering (Hebrews 5:8).

3. **He had learned to be obedient in small things**. We have seen how some of his experiences taught him that God requires faithfulness in detail.

Through the obedience of this man Moses, the people are going to experience God's salvation. It was the same in the case of Jesus. Jesus never sinned. It was 'through the obedience of one man' that 'the many will be made righteous' (Romans 5:19).

Now there comes a series of judgements upon Pharaoh. They are designed to force Pharaoh to release Israel. There are ten of them: the turning of water into blood, the frogs, the gnats, the flies, the plague on the livestock, the boils, the hail, the locusts, the thick darkness, and finally the death of the firstborn. The miracles of judgement produced no release for Israel, for during the first nine judgements Pharaoh refuses to yield. They were saved not by the miraculous signs but by the blood of the lamb.

The judgements were warning judgements. Pharaoh was experiencing the anger of God against his sinfulness and rebelliousness. God gives many warnings to the world before He sends His final judgement and brings the world to an end. Pharaoh came to know something of God. It did not lead to faith in his heart but it brought him to acknowledge that God is real. The unbeliever knows God, instinctively, through the fact that the world he lives in is the creation of God (see Romans 1:21). But over and above the knowledge that comes to men and women through creation, there is the knowledge that comes to them through God's mighty acts. The Bible often says that God does powerful and mighty things so that men and women will get to know that He is real. God will do mighty things 'and the Egyptians will know' that Yahweh is real (see Exodus 7:5). Miracles will take place that will lead Pharaoh to know that the God of Israel is the all-powerful God (7:17), that God is unique (8:10), that God has a special relationship to His people (see 8:22–23), that He is the one-and-only God over the whole earth (9:14), that the earth is His (9:29). God would act in such a way that the whole nation of the Egyptians would know how real God is (see 14:4, 18).

Yet this knowledge is not saving knowledge. It is not knowing God in the way that the Christian may know God. It is devoid of any true reverence for God (see 9:30). The unbeliever does not know God in the way that the Christian knows God. He knows the truth but he fights against the truth.

Consider Moses' **second visit and the miracle of the staff becoming a snake** (7:8–13). Pharaoh demands a miracle; God had already told Moses and Aaron what to do (7:8–10). Moses threw his stick down and it became a snake (7:8–10). But Pharaoh refuses to believe that Moses and Aaron are authentic messengers from God. The evidence will get greater and greater but he wants to fight the truth.

All sinners have some kind of knowledge of the truth and yet prefer to believe a lie. Sometimes they know what is true but simply will not submit to what they know. Sometimes they simply deny what they know (as the snake of Genesis 3:4 knew he was lying when he said 'You will not die'). Sometimes they ignore the truth. 'They deliberately forget' (2 Peter 3:5).

When sinners resist God they may get help from evil spirits. Men empowered by evil spirits may even be able to perform demonic miracles that imitate miracles that come from the hand of God. Pharaoh's magicians could imitate some of the miracles performed through Moses (7:11–12). The magicians could also produce what seemed to be sticks of wood that could become a snake. Yet God's power was greater. The magicians did not turn the snake back into a stick of wood – which would have been more impressive! The fact that the magicians' own snakes could not be turned back into sticks of wood suggests that trickery was involved and that the magicians' 'sticks' were snakes from the beginning! However their snakes were swallowed by Moses' snake!

These events ought to persuade us that there is more that happens on planet earth than is understood by many secular-minded men and women, who often have no idea of the spiritual realm that exists in and alongside the physical realm that we see and handle. These events ought to make us careful about believing a teaching because it is accompanied by miracles; the demons can work miracles!

Miracles do not automatically soften the heart. The miracles did not soften Pharaoh's heart. God had said He would harden Pharaoh's heart (7:3) but God did not have to create any hardness. Pharaoh's heart was hard already (7:13). God just had to leave him alone and bring about the circumstances that would add to his hardness. Without faith the blessings of God are not experienced.

Chapter 10

Mocking the Gods

(Exodus 7:14–8:19)

Twice Moses had been to see Pharaoh. At first he needlessly antagonised him. Then he went again to present miraculous credentials. After that, Moses went nine more times to Pharaoh (7:15; 8:1, 16, 20; 9:1, 8, 13; 10:1, 21) and then was told never to come again (9:28–29). But after the tenth miracle took place it was not that Moses went to Pharaoh; rather Pharaoh called for Moses (12:32). Altogether he had twelve interviews with Moses.

The first miracle was that of the turning of the Nile into blood (7:14–24). Moses is sent to speak to Pharaoh about his unwillingness to hear God's demand (7:14–16). He is to work a miracle to confirm the authenticity of God's word. Moses must explain that 'Yahweh' is 'the God of the Hebrews'. He takes the staff which had been used before; this will remind Pharaoh that he had already seen signs which should convince him of the reality of God's power. The miracle was announced before it happened (7:17–18). It was designed that Pharaoh would know that 'Yahweh' was real. He had said 'Who is Yahweh?' (5:2). He is getting an answer. While Pharaoh was watching, the Nile turned to blood (7:19–21). The River Nile was the source of life and fertility for Egypt. But God could end its provisions for Egypt at any time He wished.

Pharaoh's magicians could imitate the miracle (7:22a), but they could not reverse it. Their miracles were always miracles bringing further judgement, never miracles of healing or restoration. They could not miraculously reverse God's miracle of judgement. It would have been more impressive if they had turned the blood to water! Pharaoh still resisted God's voice

(7:22b–23) although the effects of God's judgement continued for some time (7:24).

Seven days later came **the second miracle, the plague of frogs** (7:25–8:15). Again Pharaoh is told in advance what will happen (8:1–2). This time there will be greater suffering involved. There was no suffering when Moses' staff became a snake. There was some inconvenience when the Nile became blood. But now the plague of frogs will bring great disaster. The frogs will be in Pharaoh's palace, in the beds, in the places where bread is made – everywhere. The death of the frogs and the smell of dead frogs everywhere was to be a hint of what God could do if He wished to bring the life of the Egyptians to an end. The whole land will get to know what is happening (8:3–4).

The miracle takes place (8:5–6). The magicians again can imitate the miracle but they cannot reverse Moses' miracle (8:7).

There is now a hint that Pharaoh might be yielding. He summons Moses and Aaron (a thing he had not done before). He knows they can bring the judgement to an end; his magicians cannot (8:8). He promises to release Israel to worship Yahweh (something he has not done before). He agrees to let the people go if the frogs are taken away. Moses makes an offer that the timing should be chosen by Pharaoh (8:9–10a); this will make it plain that there is a sheer miracle taking place. Pharaoh will have enough evidence to convince him not only that Yahweh is real (see Exodus 7:5) and the God of Israel is the all-powerful God (see Exodus 7:17), but also that God is unique (Exodus 8:10b–11). It happens as Moses said it would. Moses is called to be an intercessor for the unsaved Pharaoh (8:12–14).

But there was no change in Pharaoh's heart. Here was all the proof he needed, but he yielded to God's word only when forced to do so. There was a mixture of knowledge and denial in his heart. He knew God was real but he refused to allow that knowledge to have any weight with him. He 'exchanged the truth of God for a lie' (Romans 1:25). He admitted that Yahweh was a God of power but his acknowledgement did him no good since it had no affect upon his heart and his will.

The third miraculous judgement was the plague of gnats

(8:16–19) or perhaps mosquitoes. God was speaking powerfully to Pharaoh. This time there was no warning.

God speaks to everyone in one way or another. All hear the voice of God in creation (Romans 1:21). Pharaoh was getting something over and above the voice of God in creation. He was seeing the hand of God in history and Moses was there to interpret what was happening. Miraculous signs were coming alongside God's word. At first Pharaoh would not yield at all. After the second miracle he was forced to acknowledge Yahweh's power.

When Moses was told to strike the ground a plague of gnats invaded the land of Egypt (8:16–17). This time the magicians could not imitate the miraculous judgement (8:18) and even the magicians were insisting 'This is the finger of God', but Pharaoh would not yield (8:19).

It is likely that these various judgements were intended to show God's power to Pharaoh; they were also ways of ridiculing the gods of Egypt. It is possible that the various plagues actually referred to the gods and goddesses of Egypt. The first plague showed the powerlessness of the god of the Nile. The second judgement ridiculed a goddess whose symbol had a frog's head – and so on.

The various gods of the world are worthy of being ridiculed and the Bible pours scorn on them. It does not mention their names. They are not even worthy of having their names mentioned! Only those who are honoured are worthy of having a name.

Moses' God can announce what is to happen and then He can do what He has said He will do.

> 'Bring the gods near and let them tell us what is going to take place!
> Declare the things that are going to come afterwards,
> That we may know that you are gods . . .
> Behold, you are less than nothing and utterly worthless!'
>
> (Isaiah 41:22–24)

God's salvation begins by ridiculing the gods. No one and nothing can act in the way He can act, and it is such a God who saves by the blood of a lamb.

Chapter 11

God's Control of the Human Heart
(Exodus 8:20–9:12)

The fourth judgement was the plague of flies (8:20–32). God was steadily producing more and more evidence of the truth of His word and the greatness of His power. Now God made it clear that Israel was special to Him, for Israel did not suffer from the plague of flies (8:20–23).

Pharaoh had been forced to know God's name, God's power and God's uniqueness. Now he will know that Yahweh specially cares for His people. This judgement is again announced a day ahead.

It happens as Moses says and for the first time Pharaoh is willing to take steps towards yielding towards God's demand. But it is an obedience that is forced out of him and he is only partially willing to do as God says. He says he will allow the Israelites to sacrifice to Yahweh while they remain in Egypt (8:24–25). Moses refuses the offer (8:26–27). Pharaoh concedes even more. They may go to the desert 'but not very far' (8:28). He now even asks for prayer. Here we have a man who is convinced of God's reality and even of the power of prayer – and yet he is not willing to put his trust in God and submit to Him. He believes the truth about God and yet believes a lie at the same time. He believes God but not in the sense of trusting God to be good to him personally.

The unbeliever is able to have considerable knowledge 'about' God and yet have no relationship to God. Soon Pharaoh gets further confirmation of God's word to him (8:29–31), but as soon as there is no great pressure for him to acknowledge God, he backs away from his promises and will not let Israel go (8:32).

It is a very striking illustration of how much a person may know that God is real and yet be unwilling to have the kind of faith that will wholeheartedly surrender to God.

The fifth judgement was the plague on the livestock of Egypt (9:1–7). Moses was sent to tell Pharaoh that if he would not release Israel a plague would come upon Egypt's domestic animals (9:1–3). The Hebrews would be spared, so it would be plain that God was treating His people in a distinct way (9:4). Again the timing was specified; it would be clear that this was an act of God (9:5). On the next day it happened as Moses had forewarned (9:6–7). This time Pharaoh specially sent investigators to find out what had happened in the area of the Israelites. But no amount of plain evidence that God is at work is enough to change Pharaoh's heart. Again he refuses Moses' request (9:7).

The sixth judgement was the plague of boils (9:8–12). Moses must throw the soot from a furnace into the air. It will become fine dust and will spread boils on the people of Egypt and upon their animals (9:8–9). This is what happens (9:10). This time the magicians were affected. Earlier, the magicians had imitated the miracles done through Moses. Then they had found that there were miracles they could not imitate. Now the miraculous judgement affects them (9:11).

'Yahweh hardened the heart of Pharaoh' (9:12). It may be noticed that the expression changes here. Before it had been said that Pharaoh's heart was hard, or that Pharaoh hardened his heart. Now it is said 'Yahweh hardened the heart of Pharaoh'. Pharaoh hardened his own heart before God did anything. When God hardened the heart of Pharaoh He was not **creating** hardness of heart. He was simply handing Pharaoh over to his own desires. God was not forcing Pharaoh to sin; He was allowing Pharaoh to have his own way.

The 'heart' is the inner personality. It is the place where we allow God to speak to us within. It is 'with the heart' that 'a person believes' (see Romans 10:9–10). It is the heart that can become 'an evil heart of unbelief' (Hebrews 3–12). Pharaoh knew in his heart that these things that Moses was saying were true. Yet he resisted the pressure of the truth upon his heart.

God hardens Pharaoh's heart by letting him have his own way and by drawing out and intensifying the wickedness that was already in him. God can do this. If we rebel against God – and we are all born rebels – He can hand us over to our own rebelliousness. Faith and repentance are gifts of God, and He does not have to give them! 'They could not believe', says John 12:39, '...He has blinded their eyes and hardened their heart...'. This does not mean that God creates sin, but He can use the sin that is already there for His own purpose. He can withdraw all restraining influences. God can hand a person over to Satan. He can take the sinner and make all the wickedness that is in him show itself. Then when sin has done its worst, God steps in and reveals the greatness of His power.

God often does this in the history of the world. He does not only work in individuals. He also works in great movements of history. Here is mighty Egypt, the most powerful kingdom in the world at the time we are considering. And within mighty Egypt is a little persecuted tribe. But the little persecuted tribe is chosen by God, and God has a purpose to use them. He lets Pharaoh do his worst. He actually brings out the greatness of Pharaoh's wickedness and malice against Israel. He rouses Pharaoh to a high pitch of hatred. God is not creating anything; He is simply drawing out what is already there. God can control the heart, even of the wicked. Why does God do this? To show the greatness of His power. He wants His people to see the pagans and their gods at the very worst, and then see that He is greater! Mighty kings and mighty nations are just a 'drop from a bucket ... a speck of dust on the scales' (Isaiah 40:15).

Chapter 12

The Last Warnings

(Exodus 9:13–10:29)

The seventh judgement was the destructive hailstorm (9:13–35). Heavy hail with thunder and lightning ruined the barley in upper Egypt but not in Goshen. God is increasing the severity of His judgement against Pharaoh. How great will the chastising punishment of God have to be before Pharaoh will yield? God warns Pharaoh, 'I will send the full force of my plagues'. God will compel Pharaoh to recognise God's uniqueness (9:13–14). God could have removed Pharaoh from existing on earth altogether (9:15). But God has raised Pharaoh up to his position in history in order to demonstrate His power (9:16). God has actually been restraining His anger. He has endured Pharaoh with much longsuffering. But God has used the wickedness of Pharaoh. God can use sin in order to achieve some purpose of His own. It is this verse that Paul quotes in Romans 9:17. The point is that God's purpose is not **failing** because of Pharaoh. Far from it. Pharaoh is in fact raised up by God to be used by God in His purpose. God plans to give a magnificent demonstration of His power. He uses Pharaoh's sinful hardness to achieve not Pharaoh's will but His own will.

This is a constant theme of Scripture. In a mysterious way, sin does not achieve its own will; it achieves God's will. This does not mean that God creates sin, but it does mean that God so controls sin that it does not achieve its own will. Hail was an extremely rare event; Egypt received almost no rain. Pharaoh is still in rebellion against God (9:17), so a miraculously timed and miraculously heavy hailstorm is about to come (9:18). It threatened death to human life and to all domestic animals (9:19). The prediction forced a separation between those who did and those who did not believe in Moses' predictions (9:20–21).

The violent hailstorm comes as predicted (9:22–25). Israel's territory in Goshen was spared (9:26). Pharaoh relents more than he had done before. He admits to sin (9:27), asks for Moses to pray for him and promises to let the Hebrews go (9:28).

Moses promises to intercede (9:29) and Pharaoh will be forced to know that the earth belongs to Yahweh, the God of Israel, but Pharaoh's knowledge does not lead to the fear of God (29:30). Pharaoh now has **knowledge**, but he does not have **respect** for God. The 'natural man' in some sense 'knows God' and may be brought to a yet greater knowledge of God. But a reluctant willingness to admit that God is real and that God is powerful is not enough to bring about a heart-felt loving submission to God. Knowledge is forced upon Pharaoh but it has not led to a change of heart, or a change in the direction of his life.

The agriculture of Egypt was severely damaged, although the survival of the wheat and spelt (9:31–32) meant that there was some mercy amidst God's judgement. As soon as the pressure was off of Pharaoh, the true state of his heart was revealed; he still had not submitted to God (9:33–35). What God wants is not knowledge but submission. One may know a great deal about God and his ways but have an un-submissive heart.

The eighth judgement was the plague of locusts (10:1–20). Again God gives Moses a preview of what is about to happen. The signs that God will give will be forever remembered by the people of Israel (10:1–2). Pharaoh is persistently proud and disobedient (10:3). God will now send an unprecedented plague of locusts (10:4–6). Almost everyone in Egypt now knows the power of God and the trustworthiness of Moses' word. They implore Pharaoh to yield to God's will (10:7). Pharaoh is willing to let Israel go but only if he keeps the children in Egypt (10:8–11). Soon the judgement of God comes (10:12–15) and Pharaoh is forced to pretend obedience once again (10:16) and to plead for 'this death' (10:17) to be taken away. In response to Moses' intercession God took the chastening punishment away in an impressively thorough manner (10:18–19), but God hardened Pharaoh's heart (10:20) and again the permission to leave was withdrawn.

The ninth judgement was the darkness over the land. At Moses' signal there came a thick darkness over the land (10:21–22). It was probably a whirlwind spreading thick dust, so thick that it blotted out the light of the sun. Israel was excepted (10:23). Pharaoh agrees to the release of Israel (10:24–26), but God hardens his heart and Pharaoh withdraws his permission (10:27). The series of interviews is brought to an end by Pharaoh himself. He – in his own hardness of heart which has been confirmed by God – makes the decision that he wishes to have no more of these interviews with Moses who has been to him the agent of God's word coming to him (10:28–29).

God had demonstrated His total and absolute control over the so-called gods of Egypt and over every kind of natural phenomena. He had brought these things to pass with ever-increasing severity. Pharaoh had made it clear that his rebelliousness was in the face of clear proof of the reality of Yahweh, and he had himself admitted that Yahweh was behind what had been happening. He himself was now refusing to see Moses again. He was himself bringing to an end his opportunities to know God. *'Get out of my sight'* (Exodus 10:29) is the last word to Moses, and it reveals the final state of Pharaoh's heart.

God's judgements are preceded by warnings. Final judgement came only slowly upon Pharaoh and after very many warnings and clear indications of God's will. It is a great mistake to withstand God's voice. At any point Pharaoh could have said 'I am wrong' but God let him have the kind of heart that he wanted – one that was totally hardened against God.

These warnings are Pharaoh's last chance. There comes a time when God does not speak again. Now will come God's tenth judgement. It will be quite different from the other nine. For every sinner there is a last opportunity, the time after which God will never give the same opportunity again.

Chapter 13

Salvation and Judgement
(Exodus 11:1-10)

The tenth judgement was the death of the firstborn sons. God was adopting Israel as His son. The entire people were God's firstborn. Since Pharaoh was refusing to release the nation of Israel, God's firstborn son, God announced that His tenth judgement would be the death of firstborn sons throughout Egypt. It is this tenth judgement that will lead to the release of the people.

There is no change of scene between Exodus 10 and Exodus 11. Moses is still standing before Pharaoh where we left him at the end of chapter 10. God will bring one more plague, and it will lead to radical, total and permanent release from the bondage of Egypt (11:1).

When God saves us He does so radically. It is not that we are left where we are but get a little bit of help from God. God did not leave the Israelites in Egypt but just gave them a little bit of help. Rather when God saves us He takes us altogether out of the realm where we once were and takes us to a different realm altogether. In the story of the Exodus the transfer was territorial. The people were rescued from Egypt and the nation was brought eventually to Canaan. With the Christian the change is spiritual. God transfers us out of the kingdom of darkness into the kingdom of Jesus. It is important to see salvation this way. It is a **transfer of kingdoms** not just a little bit of religion!

In this transfer from one territory to another, Israel will receive ample provision. The people are going to ask for supplies from their neighbours and they will receive it in abundance. The Egyptians will be glad to give assistance in releasing Israel to a new destiny (11:2). There will be favour from God, but favour from the people as well (11:3).

There will be a final judgement. In every family the firstborn son will die by the direct and supernatural hand of God. The nine earlier plagues could be regarded as simply unusual incidents in the course of nature. They involved remarkable events in the physical territory of the land of Egypt with its river, its insects, its animals and its sunshine. But now there comes something greater, the direct hand of God. In this judgement Moses will not use his staff (as in 7:19 and elsewhere) or stretch out his hand (as in 10:21). God says *'I will bring one more plague . . . About midnight I will go throughout Egypt'* (11:4).

The judgement will be universal. Every household in Egypt will experience God's action, from Pharaoh to the humblest slave (11:5). Even the firstborn animals will die. As in the story of the flood the created universe is tied in with the human race. When people are judged, their possessions are judged as well.

The judgement will bring extreme distress. There will be an unprecedented wailing of bereavement throughout the land (11:6).

Amidst the judgement there will be salvation. The salvation will be for God's people whom He has determined to save. There is a people 'chosen by grace' (as Paul would say). For no reason in themselves God has resolved to take Israel to Himself as a chosen nation. It has nothing to do with Israel's merits. Israel did not choose itself, nor were they distinguished for their great devotion to God. It is Yahweh who 'makes a distinction between Egypt and Israel'. As a nation Israel is chosen according to grace. No reason can be given for the choice of the nation except God's will. It was not because of anything Israel had done but because of God's own purpose and grace (compare 2 Timothy 1:9).

The salvation for Israel would be comprehensive and far-reaching. Not a dog would bark against them (11:7). Their deliverance would be profound, far greater than anything they could have dreamt of in those days when they 'groaned in their slavery and cried out' (see 2:23).

For Israel their release would be effortless. It would not be a matter of sneaking out in timidity and fear. They would not have to beg to be released. It would not take mammoth efforts. The officials of Pharaoh would submit to Moses and the people would be publicly, officially, released (11:8a).

All of this was told to Pharaoh before the event. There was opportunity for Pharaoh to call for mercy. But there was no sign of any willingness to change in Pharaoh, even though his own firstborn son was threatened by this latest announcement. The total unconcern of Pharaoh and his disbelief despite the many evidences that have been presented to him rouses Moses' anger (11:8b). He sees immense suffering awaiting the people of Egypt. The total refusal to take warning or show any concern for the suffering that awaits the land of Egypt arouses Moses' anger. Moses is a man of compassion. Pharaoh's relentless cruelty in having no concern for the sufferings of his people fills Moses with distress (11:8b). Moses announces all this to Pharaoh but it produces no change in his attitude. As God had said, he still would not let the people go. Yahweh had inflamed within him his own hardness of heart.

All the principles of the Christian's salvation are to be found here. God's judgement is still universal. He looks upon every member of the human race and weighs their sins and their refusal to hear His voice. God's judgements bring extreme distress. Yet amidst God's judgement there is salvation. God is still a God who takes a people to Himself, separating them out from all others. Still it has nothing to do with merit. It is because of God's own purpose and grace. Still salvation is comprehensive and far-reaching. If God is for us who can be against us? Who shall separate us from the love of Christ. Still God's salvation is in its beginnings effortless, received not worked for, given not deserved.

Chapter 14

The Lamb of God
(Exodus 12:1–6)

God is about to bring the Israelites to the land of Canaan as He had promised (see Genesis 15:13–14). At the same time God is giving Israel a picture of the way in which He sends salvation by the blood of the lamb. The passover gives the principles of salvation which would later operate in and through the blood of Jesus. Exodus 12:1–13:16 tells of the original events. Other vital references to the subject in the Old Testament are Exodus 34:25; Leviticus 23:5; Numbers 9:1–14; 28:16; 33:3; Deuteronomy 16:1–8; Joshua 5:10–11; 2 Chronicles 30:1–27 and the two accounts of the same event that we find in 2 Kings 23:21–23 and 2 Chronicles 35:1–19.

The event of passover was to be ever remembered in Israel. The calendar would start at its anniversary. *'This month is to be for you the first month'* (see 12:1–2). From now on Israel's year would begin in the month which commemorated the deliverance by the blood of the lamb.

God's judgement is about to come into the land of Egypt but there is a way of salvation. On the tenth day of the month, each family is to take a lamb. Some sharing might take place but every family or group of families joining together was to have a lamb (12:3–4). The lamb had to be young, healthy, male and without any defect (12:5). On the fourteenth day the entire nation would sacrifice 'the lamb' at twilight (12:6).

Salvation is to take place by the sacrifice of a substitute. God is about to save Israel but God's salvation takes place by a lamb being killed instead of the firstborn. Salvation does not come about by God's ignoring the problem of sin. It is not that God says to Israel 'I'll judge Egypt for its sins but in your case I'll just forget the whole matter!' No, salvation does not come by God's forgetfulness or neglect. It is not that God simply and purely withholds the punishment of sin in the case of His people. It does not work like that.

Rather Israel's sins are punished in the lamb. Israel is punished for its sins as much as the Egyptians are punished for their sins. The only difference is that in the case of Israel the punishment falls on the lamb. The judgement of God against sin is not brushed aside. Instead it falls elsewhere.

Israel had sinned as much as Egypt. Israel were sinners too! Pharaoh had refused to hear Moses. But there were times when Israel refused to hear Moses. On one occasion the Bible says 'The Israelites did not listen to him' (6:9). And there would be many times in the future when Israel would criticise Moses and refuse to heed him. Pharaoh refused to listen out of the unbelief of his rebelliousness. The Israelites often refused to listen out of the deep unbelief that had come through their great discouragement. All have sinned, and come short of the glory of God. Israel was also about to experience the falling of the wrath of God, but it will be turned aside to fall upon the lamb that God has provided. The lamb is a substitute. The lamb dies instead of the firstborn sons of Israel.

This helps us to understand the cross of our Lord Jesus Christ. Salvation still comes by the death of a substitute. Jesus died instead of us. He carried the anger of God against sin instead of us ourselves having to carry the anger of God against sin. Yet when God forgives the sins of His people, He is not changing His mind about punishing sin. He **still** punishes sin – only He punishes it in another, in our Lord Jesus Christ.

Salvation does not come because God's people are worthy of salvation. Far from it. They have been sinners as much as anyone else. And salvation does not come by God's somehow neglecting His wrath in the case of His people. No! God saves by atonement. God saves by providing a substitute. God saves by the blood of the lamb.

Jesus is God's lamb. He is 'the lamb of God', as John the Baptist called him (John 1:29, 36). He is provided by God. **The provision of a sacrifice for sins is God's idea**. It was God who put forward this way of salvation. It was not Moses' idea or the people's idea. 'Christ our passover has been sacrificed', said the apostle Paul (1 Corinthians 6:7). 'He was led like a lamb to the slaughter', says Isaiah 53:7, speaking of the predicted Suffering Servant of God. 'God himself will provide the lamb for the burnt offering', said Abraham when talking to his son Isaac (Genesis 22:8), and the same principle applies in the passover that saved Israel, and in the cross of Jesus Christ which saves us. God provided the lamb.

The lamb had to be perfect. Jesus had to be sinless. Jesus would never have been able to save us if He had been a sinner. He took the place of sinners but He was not a sinner himself. One sinner cannot bring salvation for another sinner. Jesus had to be 'without spot or blemish' if He was to be our Saviour.

The lamb had to die. There was no salvation through the lamb until the lamb had died. The producing of the blood was the proof that the lamb had died. Our salvation does not come by our imitating the earthly life of Jesus. Nor does our salvation come simply by our accepting the teaching of Jesus. Our salvation comes by the death of Jesus. We are 'justified by his blood' (Romans 5:9); it is through 'the blood of his cross' (Colossians 1:20). We are 'made near by the blood of Christ', says Ephesians 2:13. He has 'loosed us from our sins by his blood', says Revelation 1:5.

In the days of the passover God was bringing salvation in the same way that He would bring it through Jesus. All have sinned, but God's salvation consists in the death of a substitute. We have 'redemption through his blood' (Ephesians 1:7).

Chapter 15

The Blood of the Lamb
(Exodus 12:7–11)

God was about to judge the entire land of Egypt, including Goshen where the people of Israel were living. Every individual was under judgement but the firstborn would represent the entire family. Yet in the midst of the judgement there was a way of salvation. God provided a lamb as a substitute. For some, the lamb would die instead of them. For those firstborn members of the family who sheltered under the blood of the passover lamb, there would be safety.

The lamb dies instead of the people. It is not that God forgets their sins. There is a judgement in Goshen. God does not ignore His people's sins; He judges them in a substitute. God provided Jesus, His lamb. Jesus was punished for sin instead of the human race.

The story emphasises the blood. After the lamb had been killed in each family they had to take the blood and put it on the doorposts and the top of the door so that blood was painted all around the doorway (12:7). The blood had to be produced explicitly. There were other ways to kill an animal (strangling, for example), but the blood had to be produced to prove the animal had died in bloody sacrifice.

The blood was not painted on the floor of the doorway. The blood was not to be 'trodden underfoot' (see Hebrews 10:29).

The people were to gather on the fourteenth day. The lamb would be killed. The blood would be painted around the doorway, and then the lamb would be eaten. Each family or group of small families would eat 'the lamb'. It was spoken of as if it were just one lamb.

The lamb had to be roasted (12:8). At the same time as the eating of the animal, some other foods were to be eaten as well. Unleavened bread and bitter herbs were taken with the meat of the lamb (12:8). The entire animal had to be roasted whole (12:9). They were not allowed to leave aside the head or the thighs of the animal. Not a bone was to be broken (compare John 19:36).

Leaven represented impurity. It is 'leaven' or 'yeast' which makes the dough ferment. It was used sometimes as a picture of impurity or corruption. Bitter herbs represented the sufferings and bitter life the Hebrews had endured (Exodus 1:14). They were being redeemed from the bitter experience of bondage.

As the Israelites ate the lamb they were not to leave anything of the lamb remaining. Anything that was not edible or was left uneaten had to be consumed with fire (12:10).

As they ate the roast lamb on that first passover night they were to be dressed ready for an abrupt and sudden journey. They had a belt around their waist so that they could walk rapidly without their flapping robes making them walk slower. They had their sandals on their feet. They were to have a staff in their hand. And they were to eat rapidly, not leisurely.

Every aspect of this event spoke of God's way of salvation. Jesus was a sacrifice for our sins on the cross. Jesus did not die of illness or of old-age. He died under the judgement of God. It was a terrible death. It was violent and ugly. He was abandoned by people and abandoned by God. There is a lot of emphasis in the Bible on blood. Our salvation takes place by the blood-sacrifice of Jesus. This is why the New Testament often speaks of the blood of Christ (Matthew 26:28; Luke 22:20; John 6:53–56; 19:34; Acts 20:28; Romans 3:25; 5:9; 1 Corinthians 10:16; 11:25, 27; Ephesians 1:7; 2:13; Colossians 1:14, 20; Hebrews 9:14; 10:19, 29; 13:12; 1 Peter 1:2, 19; 1 John 1:7; 5:6, 8; Revelation 1:5; 5:9; 7:14; 12:11; 17:6). 'Blood' means death as a sacrifice for sins.

If the Israelites' firstborn children would shelter under the blood, all would be well for them. They would be kept safe. If we shelter under the blood of Jesus Christ the judgement of God will pass by us without destroying us. It happens now. At this very moment the wrath of God is averted for all who trust Jesus and we are taken as God's children. It will happen also at the final judgement day. When the unsaved are experiencing the anger of God the saved will find that the wrath of God will pass them by again. They will be safe because of the blood of the lamb.

The story emphasises the speed at which their salvation takes place. They had wanted to escape Egypt for many years but had not been able to find deliverance. They had prayed to go, but nothing brought them release. Even the previous nine miraculous judgements had not led to Pharaoh's letting the people go. But the blood can do what nothing else could do. Once the lamb has died and the people have fed on it they are free! Before they could not get out of Egypt. Now they cannot stay in! Immediately they are pilgrims travelling to a new land. Instantly they are freed. The unleavened bread was easily and speedily cooked. It meant they could leave swiftly, urgently.

The unleavened bread spoke of urgency in leaving behind the old wicked, sinful, painful life. In 1 Corinthians 5:7 Paul said 'Clean out the old leaven ... Christ our passover is sacrificed'. The passover lamb pictures Jesus. The leaven is a picture of the old life from which Jesus delivers us.

They were never to forget this day. The bitter herbs would be a reminder of the painful days that had experienced before. The Christian remembers the days when he was without Jesus. He looks back on them with horror. 'Never again will I go back to that!' he says to himself.

The Israelites were to make a meal of the lamb. The lamb which had died for them became afterwards the source of their strength, their energy, their life. This is the way to forgiveness. We shelter beneath the blood of the lamb. This is the way to live. We get strength from the Lamb.

Chapter 16

Sheltering Under the Blood
(Exodus 12:12–13)

Salvation is by the blood of the lamb. God demands it and God provided it. God insisted that He would come through the land of Egypt and there would be judgement in each household. The firstborn was the representative of the family. God was about to let the wages of sin fall in each family in Egypt. God was insisting on the shedding of blood as the wages of sin.

Yet God supplied the blood which He demanded. Instead of the firstborn, God provided the blood of a substitute. In the place of the firstborn the lamb would die instead.

It is exactly in this way that the New Testament speaks of Jesus 'the lamb of God' (John 1:29). The New Testament doctrine of the atonement is a Jesus-centred reinterpretation of the story of the exodus. God put forward a substitute, Jesus.

God was giving a demonstration of how He saves. He was giving a way of interpreting what He would do through His Son. When Jesus came, the people of Israel would know about a lamb dying for the sins of the people. The passover ceremony was to be kept as an annual reminder of the original passover. It would prepare the people for Jesus. He was the one who would bear the wrath of God against sin instead of us. He is the lamb. The judgement of God passes us by because Jesus has died. Jesus died at passover time. It was quite deliberate. The rulers said 'Not at the festival' (Matthew 26:5). They wanted to avoid Jesus' dying at passover time. But God overruled and Christ died on the Friday at passover time. He was a passover-sacrifice Himself, dying for the sins of the people.

1. **God wants the blood**. God is holy and just. He requires that a death-penalty should fall because of sin. He needs to

express His holy hatred against sin. The blood is first for God. 'When I see the blood, I will pass over you', says God (12:13). The blood is first of all for God. He is looking for it. When He sees it He turns aside His wrath.

2. **God provided the blood**. The whole idea of the passover came from God. It was not a device of Moses or any man or any woman. It was wholly God's idea. It is God who tells Moses about what He has provided. It is God who gives the instructions about the lamb. It is God who announces His judgement. 'I will ... strike down every firstborn ... ' (12:12). It is God who tells what the blood will do. *'I will pass over you. No destructive plague will touch you ... '* (12:13).

It as the same with Jesus. God needed that Jesus should die. There had to be atonement. There had to be a judgement against sin.

Yet at the same time as God demanded the penalty against sin, He also loved us. God 'so loved the world' (John 3:16). God 'commended his love' (Romans 5:8). The idea of providing an atonement for sin came out of the heart of God the Father. He demanded that sin should be dealt with. He also provided that the penalty should be carried by Another. He was recommending His love. God loved the human race yet could not relinquish the punishment of sin. Jesus the lamb of God was God's remedy. He transferred the penalty to Another and provided His own Lamb.

3. **God required faith**. The blood of the lamb was not totally automatic. The God who judges sin was also putting forward the lamb to bear the judgement, yet there was one thing that had to happen if any firstborn son or daughter was to be actually saved. They had to believe what God was saying. They had to trust that the lamb had actually died for them, and they had to be sure to shelter under the blood of the lamb by going within the house whose doorway was marked by blood.

Israelite nationality counted for nothing. There might be an Israelite firstborn son wandering around outside on that first passover night. 'I am an Israelite', he might say to himself. 'Surely God would not punish one of His chosen people'. But Israelite nationality was not what God was demanding. He demanded faith shown by sheltering under the blood of the lamb.

The level of good living counted for nothing. There might be a very good living Israelite firstborn son wandering around outside on that first passover night. 'I am a good person', he might say. 'Surely God would not punish me'. But high morality was not what God was demanding. He demanded faith shown by sheltering under the blood of the lamb.

Intellectual comprehension counted for nothing. There might be someone who said 'I do not understand it. Why should protection from the judgement of God come in this way?' But it was irrelevant whether what was happening was understood or not. What saved was not theology but faith.

The blood of Jesus Christ is the basis of our assurance of salvation. You might want to ask 'How can I **know** I will be saved from God's anger against sin?' The blood of Jesus Christ is the answer. *'When I see the blood . . . I will pass over you'* said God (Exodus 12:13). Let the blood of Jesus Christ be enough for you. It is enough for God! Let it be enough for you. Believe it. Trust your whole life to the blood of Jesus Christ. Let nothing make you doubt. Do not hold back or try to prepare yourself in some way. Take shelter under the blood of Jesus Christ and you will be saved. Then you will be in a position to call out to God as His child. Then you will be in a position to call out to God for the gift of His Holy Spirit. The starting point of everything is to take shelter under the blood of Jesus Christ, the lamb of God.

Chapter 17

Bought with a Price

(Exodus 12:14–20)

Before the description of what happened on passover night, the story speaks of the demand that from this point on 'Passover' will be an annual ceremony in Israel (12:14), accompanied by the Feast of Unleavened Bread (12:15–20).

According to Exodus 12:14–20 God gives instructions concerning the Feast of Unleavened Bread.

In Exodus 12:21–27 Moses gives instructions concerning the present (12:21–23) and the future (12:24–27) passover.

Exodus 12:28–30 tells of the death of the firstborn.

According to Exodus 12:31–34, Pharaoh sends away the Israelites.

According to Exodus 12:35–36, the Israelites plunder the Egyptians.

Exodus 12:37–39 tells of the journey from Rameses to Succoth.

1. **First, God looks to the future and tells them they must never forget that this passover is the central event of their history**. The greatest and most important thing that will ever happen to them is about to take place, the day of their being redeemed with the blood of a lamb. This was the very meaning of God's name 'Yahweh'.

From now on 'Passover' would be an annual festival-time in Israel. It would be a 'memorial' calling upon them never to forget what happened to them at this time. It would be a regular reminder of what had happened at the time of their becoming 'Israel', at the first passover (12:14). At the first passover there was little time to celebrate. But at the annual passover-festival the one day of Passover celebration would be followed by

a whole week keeping the Feast of Unleavened Bread
(12:15). The two feasts together would celebrate what God
had done.

The Christian must apply this idea to the blood of Jesus
Christ. The cross, the 'blood of the lamb', is the central event of
Christian history. Jesus Himself steadfastly set Himself to go to
Jerusalem to die. The four Gospels emphasise the cross more
than anything else in their story. Paul refused to 'glory' in
anything other than the cross (Galatians 6:14). The Christian
gospel is a matter of 'Christ and him crucified' (1 Corinthians
2:2) before it is anything else. Our central emphasis must not be
prosperity or healing or miracles or social welfare or anything
other than Jesus and His blood. The event that is never to be
forgotten and is to be 'placarded' or 'publicly portrayed'
(Galatians 3:1) is the blood of the lamb.

2. **Redemption by blood purifies the people and consecrates
them to God**. At this point in the story the book of Exodus
inserts detailed instructions concerning the keeping of the Feast
of Unleavened Bread (12:15–20). At the time of the first
passover-event the people were to eat only bread which was
without leaven and could be cooked at speed. This spoke of the
haste and the urgency with which they would leave Egypt.
Nothing that took a long time to cook – such a bread with yeast
in it – was to be allowed. The roasting of the lamb would be the
only thing that took any time, and they were preparing for that
days ahead.

The Hebrews were to make an abrupt and total break with
their past life. It was to happen sharply and hurriedly. The
unleavened bread was a sign that they were not planning to
hang around.

This is how it came about that leaven symbolised the old life.
Because of what happened at this time leaven came to symbol-
ise lingering in the old life. Leaven would from now on be
forbidden in any offerings to God (see Exodus 23:18; 34:25;
Leviticus 2:11; 6:17, and the rest of the Mosaic law). It could be
eaten in everyday life or in those parts of the sacrifices that were
given for ordinary food (see Leviticus 7:13; 23:17) but in what
was offered directly to God it was forbidden.

Leaven is generally a symbol of impurity. Paul is referring to the sin of legalism when he says 'A little leaven leavens the whole lump' (Galatians 5:9). A small amount of sin can ferment and grow, like yeast in dough. Paul makes the same point in 1 Corinthians 5:6 and goes on to say 'Cleanse out the old leaven, that you may be a new lump of dough ... Christ our Passover also has been sacrificed. Therefore let us keep the feast, not with the old leaven of malice and wickedness, but with the unleavened bread of sincerity and truth' (1 Corinthians 5:7–8). Those who have been redeemed by the blood of God's Lamb, Jesus, must also learn the lesson of the Unleavened Bread. We are to cleanse out the characteristics of the old life.

In the Feast of Unleavened Bread, any bread with yeast or leaven in it would be removed from the house. For seven days only unleavened bread would be eaten. The first day and the last day were days of total rest, like the keeping of the sabbath (12:16). The blood of the lamb leads to total consecration to God. It enables us to 'enter into rest', that is, to achieve God's promises in our life such that He blesses us so powerfully that we find it restful. The 'Feast of Unleavened Bread' was to be kept permanently as a time of celebration in the future history of Israel. The Passover and the Feast of Unleavened Bread both pointed back to one day in the story of Israel. 'This very day I brought your hosts out of the land of bondage' (12:17). The double festival would be kept for eight days. Anyone who refused to align themselves with what God had done in the first passover was to lose recognition as a member of Israel, the national people of God (12:18–20). Jesus is our passover lamb. Because Jesus has shed His blood, the Christian purges out the remains of his old life. By precious blood the Christian is 'bought with a price' (1 Corinthians 6:20). He lives as a person bought with the blood of Jesus. He lives knowing that he was 'not redeemed with perishable things ... but with the precious blood of Christ, as of a lamb unblemished and spotless, the blood of Christ' (1 Peter 1:19).

Chapter 18

The Great Deliverance
(Exodus 12:21–49)

1. **God is a great Deliverer**. Moses repeats the instructions, already given by God, concerning how the first passover in Egypt will take place (12:21–23). Hyssop (a tree with leafy branches) will be used to put the blood around the door frames. No one is to take himself away from the shelter of the blood (12:22). There will be no safety anywhere except under the blood (12:23). The 'destroyer', an angel representing God, will come (12:23).

Moses goes on to say how this event will be celebrated in Israel's future life (12:24–27). It will be a family affair with the children asking a question about what happened on this famous day in their history. Then the father will give an exposition of what it means for Israel to have been saved by the blood of the lamb.

Next comes the description of the death of the firstborn (12:28–30). The people killed the lamb as they had been told (12:28) and then the destroying angel came and the firstborn children and animals of the entire land were struck down (12:29), to the great distress of the people of Egypt (12:30). God punishes sin and delivers His people at the same time.

Pharaoh at last sends away the Israelites (12:31–34). Moses did not come to Pharaoh on his own initiative (see 10:28–29) but Pharaoh sent for him! Pharaoh totally releases the people (12:30–32). From the earliest days of his being sent to Egypt, God had told Moses that this is what would happen (see 3:20), and now God's word is being fulfilled. Pharaoh actually asks for Moses to pray for him (12:32). The people of Egypt add their plea that the Israelites should leave (12:33).

2. **God's deliverance requires response**. God had told the Israelites to be ready to leave hurriedly and now they are abruptly and suddenly asked to go. They take dough which they were about to bake for the journey, and large pieces of cloth which were normally used for wrap-around clothing were now used to carry their ovens (12:34).

As God had predicted, they went out amply supplied with gifts and resources for the future. They asked for supplies from the Egyptians and they got what they asked for (12:35–36).

The first stage of the journey takes them from Rameses to Succoth (12:37–39). There are six hundred clans (as a likely translation of 12:37 has it).[1] They went with a mixed multitude.

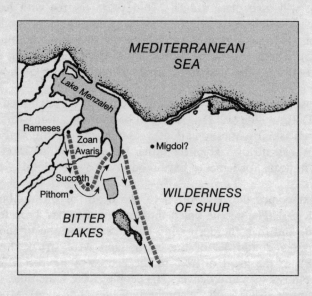

It was not nationality that saved Israel from the destroying angel; it was faith. From the beginning there were non-Israelite believers (12:38). It took faith to leave Egypt and go with Israel (see Hebrews 11:29). It was 'by faith' they crossed the Reed Sea (as it should be called). The were some gentile believers with Israel right from the start. The promise always was for 'all the families of the earth' (Genesis 12:3).

3. **God's deliverance leads to a new life**. The people went in
great haste (12:39). They travelled southwards first, reaching
places called Succoth and Etham. Later they would turn north
towards an area where there were several great lakes, and inlets
of water from the sea. One of them was the 'Sea of Reeds'.

4. **God's redemption is a great sample of His goodness and
faithfulness**. Exodus 12:40–42 comments on the greatness of the
event. Abraham's descendants had been in Egypt for about 430
years (from about 1710 to about 1280 BC; but some scholars
put it earlier). God had wonderfully preserved the descendants
of Abraham, and of Joseph, and had watched over them for
four centuries. God had told Abraham they would be away
from Canaan for about four centuries (Genesis 15:13). Now
came the time for the fulfilment of the promise (Exodus 12:41).
It was to be remembered in the following centuries (12:42).
Salvation is by the blood of Jesus. It is sprinkled around our life
and gives us protection. The cross was predicted in some detail
by Jesus just as the death of the lamb was by Moses. No one is
to take himself away from the shelter of the blood of Jesus.
There will be no safety anywhere except under the blood. The
cross of Jesus is to be explained within the family. Once we are
redeemed we are released from our old life of bondage. God
abundantly meets our needs, perhaps using even old enemies to
do so. We leave the old life abruptly and sharply. It is not
nationality that saves; people of every kind are invited to come
with us. God will wonderfully preserve us and keep all His
promises to us.

5. **The day of deliverance is to be ever remembered (12:43–49)**.
The regulations for the festival of Passover are now presented.
The feast of the Passover on the fourteenth of the month was
immediately followed by the Feast of Unleavened Bread
(Exodus 34:18, 25 treats them as two festivals). Passover was
kept on the night of the 14th Nisan; the Feast of Unleavened
Bread was kept during 15th to 21st Nisan (see also Leviticus
23:5–6; Numbers 28:16–17; Deuteronomy 16:1–8; 2 Chronicles
35:1, 17; many passages of Scripture link the two). Once a year
the Israelites were to recall the greatest miracle of the their
history – their original redemption by the blood of a lamb.

Passover was unique to Israel; no foreigner could take part unless he accepted Israel's faith (12:43–45). It was to take place on the day of the full moon, on the 14th day. That month was to be the first month of the calendar. At first the month was called 'Abib'; later it was called Nisan. On the tenth day a year-old male lamb would be selected. On the 14th Nisan 'between the two evenings' (that is, at dusk) the lamb would be killed. The blood would be applied to the doorframes of the houses, using a branch of a 'hyssop' (a leafy plant). The lamb was to be wholly roasted. No bones were to be broken (12:46). Every Israelite had to be involved (12:47). Bitter herbs would be eaten. Any remains were to be burnt. The meal was to be eaten with the participants dressed as though ready for a hasty journey. After the first events Passover was to be kept every year by all Israelites (12:47). Slaves and resident foreigners were expected to join in (12:48). Anyone was welcome to look back in faith to the blood of the lamb. Within the believers, at this point, there was to be no discrimination (12:49).

The original passover in Egypt would be kept in the peoples' homes. Later the Passover was celebrated at a central sanctuary (see Exodus 23:14–17; Deuteronomy 16:1–8) but it was not meant to lose its family-atmosphere. It was to be celebrated as a family celebration. Although the people would eventually come to Jerusalem – after the days of David – even then it would be kept in people's houses (see Matthew 26:17). The law of Moses also would allow for a minor Passover one month later for those who were ceremonially unclean at the time of the main Passover (see Numbers 9:1–14; 2 Chronicles 30:2).

Note

[1] The translation 'six hundred thousand' (here and in Numbers 11:21) is probably not right. The Hebrew *'eleph'* may mean a 'thousand' but there is reason to think it has other meanings, including 'clan' (as in Judges 6:15). The number was small enough for them to camp around the oases of Kadesh-Barnea (see Deuteronomy 1:46). It was less than the Canaanites (Exodus 23:29). Possibly the number at the time of the exodus was about 30,000 people. Still, the deliverance of 30,000 was miraculous enough!

Chapter 19

The Dedication of the Firstborn
(Exodus 12:50–13:16)

Exodus 12:50–51 lets us know that the people responded to the instructions of God and of Moses. They were a weak people, as we shall see, but they were a people of faith at this point.

After the great deliverance God requires that His people dedicate themselves to Him. There are two feasts and one ceremony that have been specially laid upon Israel at this time: the Passover, the Feast of Unleavened Bread and now the Dedication of the Firstborn.

The idea of dedicating the firstborn son and firstborn animals has several ideas in it. (i) The firstborn was to be regarded as specially belonging to God. In pagan circles human sacrifice of the firstborn sometimes took place (as the king of Moab sacrificed his son to the god Chemosh, 2 Kings 3:27). In Israel things were done differently. (ii) The firstborn had an unshakably secure inheritance. A firstborn son could not be disinherited (see Deuteronomy 21:15–16). (iii) It included the receiving of a large inheritance. A firstborn son had a double portion of his father's inheritance. (iv) It implies authority and right to rule. A firstborn son was the ruler of the father's property. Jesus is the 'heir' of God because He rules the universe for the Father.

1. **God redeems His people in order to own His people**. Every firstborn male was to be specially consecrated to God (13:1–2). At the start of His rescue of the nation God declared that He was taking the entire nation as His 'firstborn son' (Exodus 4:22–23). Pharaoh was warned that if he did not release God's firstborn, he would lose his own firstborn son (4:23). This is what happened. God intervened in what was happening in Egypt with the specific purpose of getting a son for himself.

What gave God special right to the nation was that He had redeemed them. He had executed a generation of firstborn sons and firstborn animals in Egypt in order to get them as His firstborn. They had been redeemed at great price.

Now God requires that the firstborn sons of Israel be specially dedicated to Him. They are the same people who had been specially spared when the lamb died in their place. Yet they represent the whole people of Israel. God wants the firstborn sons dedicated to Him as a sign that the whole nation is a firstborn son for God.

The demand applied also to firstborn animals. His people's wealth belongs to Him as well as the people themselves. Firstborn animals were given to God as a sign that Israel's prosperity depended on Him.

The Christian does not have to go through any dedication ceremony. He is not under the Mosaic law. But the spiritual principle applies. We are owned by God. We have been bought with a price. God wants His people as a whole and each individual Christian to be a 'firstborn son'.

In Israel the life of the firstborn son could not be taken. Firstborn sons could not be sacrificed to God by being literally killed. Only pagans and Israelite idolaters practised human sacrifice. In Israel it was forbidden. The sons had to be 'redeemed' from the death penalty over them by the payment of a price. 'Clean' animals could be sacrificed. The ass which was an 'unclean' animal could not be sacrificed. It had to be redeemed (see Deuteronomy 15:19) or executed without a religious ceremony. Later the Levites would specially be given to God as a substitute for the firstborn sons of Israel (Numbers 3:11–13, 45). The firstborn sons had to be redeemed by the father's paying five shekels.

2. **Response to God's ownership starts with purging out the leaven of the old life**. Exodus 13:3–10 seem to digress to talk about the keeping of the Feast of Unleavened Bread. But it is not really a digression. It is rather showing what the 'Dedication' means in practise. The Feast of Unleavened Bread stood for the cleansing of impurities that belonged to the period of Israel's history before they were rescued from Egypt.

Israel as God's 'firstborn', a people of faith responsible for representing God to the world, must cleanse out the characteristics of their careless and sinful past. The Feast of Unleavened Bread (13:3–7) will be a constant reminder.

The connection with the day of their salvation will be maintained. When asked, the fathers will explain. *'I did this because of what Yahweh did for me'* (13:8). The dedication of the people and their purifying themselves would be a sign to others of their belonging to Yahweh. Other nations used tattoos on their hand or head (13:9) but for the Israelites dedicating themselves to God and purifying themselves from all sin would be the sign which would mark them out to others. They needed no special tattoo on their skin; their entire life was to be an announcement that they belonged to Yahweh, the God who redeems by the blood of a lamb.

Verse 9 is the first mention of the Mosaic law. As the people approach Mount Sinai pieces of legislation come to them. The earliest anticipations of the legislation to be given at Sinai come in the requirements concerning the keeping of passover, the keeping of the feast of Unleavened Bread, and the Dedication of the Firstborn.

3. **Their dedication to God is the acknowledgement of God's faithfulness**. Exodus 13:11–16 comes back to the demand that the firstborn sons and firstborn animals be specially dedicated to God. It is a response to the Lord's faithfulness. He kept His oath to Abraham (13:11). They respond with national dedication (13:12). It includes the dedication of their wealth. The animals (13:12b) could be redeemed by death or by purchase (13:13). Pagans sacrificed their sons. Israel redeemed them by purchase. Their dedication to God gave opportunity for testimony and teaching (13:14–16). It gave the father's a chance to go over the story of how the people had been saved. The children were to grow up knowing the story of salvation.

Christians fulfil these ceremonies not by ritual but by their obvious dedication to a life of obedience to the Holy Spirit of God.

Chapter 20

The Leading of God
(Exodus 13:17–14:31)

From the moment the people were redeemed by the blood of the lamb they were 'led' by God. The people of Israel were being led to the obedience of the law; they were being led to Mount Sinai. The Christian is led by the Spirit. He is being brought to the 'law of Christ', the habit of walking in the Spirit.

There are two ways in which God leads us: the internal and the external. Often when we think of God's 'leading' we are thinking of the inner prompting of God's Holy Spirit. But there is external leading as well. In Exodus 13:21 Yahweh was going before the people in a pillar of cloud by day and a pillar of fire by night.

The cloud is a manifestation of God Himself. From time to time God makes Himself visible. It is not that the very 'stuff' of God is able to be seen. This is not possible. But angels represent God so powerfully that it is as if God is being seen. Often the appearance comes as a cloud or with a cloud. 'The glory of Yahweh appeared in the cloud', says Exodus 16:10, referring to a divine appearance. 'I come to you in a thick cloud', said God on Mount Sinai (19:9; see 19:16; 25:15, 16; 34:5; 40:34–38). God appeared also as a fire. To Abraham He revealed Himself as a 'lamp of fire' (Genesis 15:17). When God appeared to Moses it was 'in a flame of fire' (Exodus 3:2). Now God appears in a pillar of fire. Soon He will appear in an entire mountain of fire (Exodus 19:18). Then the fire and the smoke will continue in the tabernacle, when it is built.

The people of God are being visibly and externally led by God Himself. The people had been redeemed. The nation of

70

Israel had been brought into being. The blood had been shed which protected them from the anger of God against sin and enabled God to enter into a relationship with the entire nation. Now we are looking at what follows. God is in relationship with them. He begins to lead them. The cloud and fire showed them the way they should go.

1. **The leading of God does not always go by the quickest route**. God did not lead Israel by the route that led along the Mediterranean Sea in the north (13:17). There was a coastal road to Canaan. It would have been most direct to go that way, but God led them into the desert to the east of Rameses (13:18). They took the bones of Joseph, who had long before expressed faith that God's future was in Canaan (13:19). They went southwards first (13:20); God was leading them (13:21) but not in the way they would have thought.

2. **The leading of God is not always straightforward**. Suddenly God instructs the people to turn around and travel towards places in the north. It is an unexpected move. God's leading does not always go in a straight line. He sometimes takes us through unexpected twists and turns. Why is the leading of God so surprising?

3. **God's leading prevents us from being tried beyond our strength**. If God had taken them along the Mediterranean coast, they would have met Philistines and they were not yet ready for that (13:17–18).

4. **God's leading gives us a demonstration of His power**. The people were told to turn around (14:1–2). It led to Pharaoh's misunderstanding (14:3) and his heart was hardened yet further (14:4). Yet it would lead to God's demonstrating His power. *'I will get glory . . . the Egyptians will know that I am Yahweh'*, says God (14:4).

So it happened (14:5). Pharaoh changed his mind (14:5) and got ready to chase the Israelites (14:6–7). He had no sensitivity to the will of God; his heart was hardened (14:8). The Egyptians chased the Israelites and came within sight of them by one of the great lakes in the area (14:9). But it would all lead to a great demonstration of God's power. God leads us in ways that demonstrate the greatness of His sovereignty.

5. **God's leading enables us to know His ways**. The people are alarmed when they see Pharaoh's armies in the distance. They are fearful (14:10) and complain against Moses (14:11) and have regrets about their leaving Egypt (14:12). Yet it was God who had led them. They could not doubt that it was His leading.

Moses continues to believe. They are to do nothing but watch to see what God will do (14:13). God will fight for them (14:14). It seems that even Moses is secretly crying out to God. 'Why are you crying out to me?', says God; the 'you' is singular and refers to Moses. It is a time not for praying but for believing and moving forward (14:15). As the people move forward a miracle takes place. Moses is told to raise his staff (14:16). Pharaoh is about to be defeated utterly (14:17–18). The angel of Yahweh appearing in a cloud comes in between them and Pharaoh (14:19). Pharaoh cannot see them and for a while is slowed down and can make no move. God is making time for something to happen (14:20). A powerful wind blows all night (14:21) and the sea is dried up. The Israelites cross over (14:22). Soon Pharaoh tries to do the same thing (14:23–31). But God is acting to save Israel; His miracle does not continue for the Egyptians. The Egyptians go in to the middle of the sea area (14:23). God throws the army into confusion (14:24–25). The waters come back (14:26–27). Pharaoh's army is annihilated (14:28). Not one remained (14:28). Israel had walked through on dry ground (14:29).

From now on the people of Israel ought to know what God is like. He is the God who rescues us when we His people are in extreme distress. Yahweh saved them and the people saw it (14:30). They saw the great power of Yahweh and they had seen that His power had come to their aid when they needed Him (14:31). God leads us so that we may get to know His ways. God's leading is surprising but He knows what He is doing.

Chapter 21

The Song of Moses
(Exodus 15:1–21)

Now we have something new in the book of Exodus – a song.
'Then Moses and the people of Israel sang this song ... ' (15:1).
There were no songs of joy when the people were in Egypt. But
when the people become utterly and totally convinced that the
enemy is defeated and they are released forever, then their faith
is confirmed (see 14:31) and they soon start singing!

Men and women are more than pure intellect. They have
feelings and warmth and affections. Men and women are not
simply machines. They do not act with pure logic. And somehow music and poetry affect us and help us express the depth of
our feelings. When we see what a great thing God has done we
want to express ourselves with exuberance! We want to sing!

'I will sing unto Yahweh
for He is highly exalted;
the horse and its rider He had hurled into the sea.
² Yahweh is my strength and song,
and He has become my salvation;
this is my God, and I will praise him;
my father's God and I will extol him.
³ Yahweh is a warrior;
Yahweh is his name.
⁴ Pharaoh's chariots and his army God has cast into the
* sea;*
and the best of his officers are drowned in the Reed Sea.
⁵ The deep waters have covered them;
they sank to the depths like a stone.
⁶ Your right hand, O Yahweh,
was majestic in power.

Your right hand, O Yahweh,
shattered the enemy.
[7] *In the greatness of your majesty*
you threw down those who opposed you.
You unleashed your burning anger;
it consumed them like stubble.
[8] *By the blast of your nostrils*
the waters piled up.
The surging waters stood firm
like a wall;
the deep waters congealed in
the heart of the sea.
[9] *The enemy boasted,*
'I will pursue, I will overtake them.
I will divide the spoils;
I will gorge myself on them.
I will draw my sword
and my hand will destroy them'.
[10] *But you blew with your breath,*
and the sea covered them.
They sank like lead
in the mighty waters.
[11] *Who among the gods is like*
you O God?
Who is like you -
majestic in holiness,
awesome in glory,
working wonders?
[12] *You stretched out your right hand*
and the earth swallowed them.

We sing about God, and everything He has done for us.

I will sing unto Yahweh . . .
[2] *Yahweh is my strength and song . . .*
[3] *Yahweh is a warrior;*
Yahweh is his name . . .
[6] *Your right hand, O Yahweh,*
Your right hand, O Yahweh . . .

The song delights in the exaltedness of God
> *...for He is highly exalted;*

The singers are determined to lift God high.
> *...I will praise him...*
> *...I will extol him...*

They delight in the totality and completeness of what God has done.
> *...the horse and its rider He had hurled into the sea.*
> *...the best of his officers are drowned in the Reed Sea.*
> *Your right hand, O Yahweh,*
> *shattered the enemy.*
> *...you threw down those who opposed you.*
> *You unleashed your burning anger;*
> *it consumed them like stubble.*

and the ease with which He did it.
> *...you blew with your breath,*
> *and the sea covered them.*
> *They sank like lead*
> *in the mighty waters.*

They speak of what God now means to them:
> *² Yahweh is my strength and song,*
> *and He has become my salvation;*
> *this is my God, and I will praise him;*
> *my father's God and I will extol him.*

They look at the character of God. He is like a warrior.
> *³ Yahweh is a warrior...*

He has engaged in a great battle for them. And He is totally victorious.
> *⁴ Pharaoh's chariots and his army God has cast into the*
> *   sea;*
> *and the best of his officers are drowned in the Reed Sea.*
> *⁵ The deep waters have covered them;*
> *they sank to the depths like a stone.*

They speak of God's great power.
> *⁶ Your right hand, O Yahweh,*
> *was majestic in power.*
> *Your right hand, O Yahweh,*
> *shattered the enemy.*

And they speak of God's kingship.

> [7] *In the greatness of your majesty*
> *you threw down those who opposed you.*
> *You unleashed your burning anger;*
> *it consumed them like stubble.*

And they speak of God's anger against sin.

> [8] *By the blast of your nostrils*
> *the waters piled up.*
> *The surging waters stood firm*
> *like a wall;*
> *the deep waters congealed in*
> *the heart of the sea.*

They sing of the weakness of human pride.

> [9] *The enemy boasted,*
> *'I will pursue, I will overtake them.*
> *I will divide the spoils;*
> *I will gorge myself on them.*
> *I will draw my sword*
> *and my hand will destroy them'.*
> [10] *But you blew with your breath,*
> *and the sea covered them.*
> *They sank like lead*
> *in the mighty waters.*

They sing of the uniqueness of God.

> [11] *Who among the gods is like*
> *you O God?*
> *Who is like you—*
> *majestic in holiness,*
> *awesome in glory,*
> *working wonders?*
> [12] *You stretched out your right hand*
> *and the earth swallowed them.*

This is what God is like. He comes to aid of His people. He seems to delay but then He acts with such great power. Eventually everything is dealt with. 'The horse and its rider' – everything! He acts dramatically. He hurls the enemy aside. He blasts the opposition into non-existence. He does this for His

people. He becomes 'My God ... my father's God'. The singers
delight in God. They want to meditate on every detail. Then
our song moves from the recent past into the future.

> [13] *In your unfailing love you will lead*
> *the people you have redeemed.*
> *In your strength you will guide them*
> *to your holy dwelling.*
> [14] *The nations will hear and tremble;*
> *anguish will grip the people of Philistia.*
> [15] *The chiefs of Edom will be terrified,*
> *the leaders of Moab will be seized with trembling,*
> *the rulers of Canaan will melt away;*
> [16] *terror and dread will fall upon them.*
> *By the power of your arm*
> *they will be as still as a stone –*
> *until your people you bought pass by.*
> [17] *You will bring them in and plant them*
> *on the mountain of your inheritance –*
> *the place, O Yahweh, which you made for your dwelling,*
> *the sanctuary, O Yahweh, your hands established.*
> *Yahweh will reign for ever and ever.*

The people look into the future. If God has acted so
wonderfully for them in the past they are confident He will act
faithfully towards them for ever after.

They are confident of God's love.

> [13] *In your unfailing love ...*

They are confident of God's power.

> *In your strength you will guide them ...*
> *By the power of your arm*
> *they will be as still as a stone ...*

They are sure of God's leading.

> *... you will lead*
> *... you will guide them ...*

They are happy to know that God has taken them as His
people. They are

> *... the people you have redeemed.*
> *... your people ...*

77

They are now confident that they will be taken to Mount Sinai.

> *. . . you will guide them*
> *to your holy dwelling.*
> [17] *You will bring them in and plant them*
> *on the mountain of your inheritance –*
> *the place, O Yahweh, which you made for your dwelling,*
> *the sanctuary, O Yahweh, your hands established . . .*

They end their song with their assurance of God's kingship.

> *Yahweh will reign for ever and ever.'*

As the great defeat of Pharaoh is taking place (15:19), Miriam spontaneously begins to sing. She takes a tambourine and soon the ladies are dancing and singing.

> *'Sing to the Lord,*
> *for He is highly exalted.*
> *The horse and its rider*
> *He has hurled into the sea.'*   (15:21)

A few months before the people had been groaning in distress. Now they are dancing with joy. The ladies have become a choir. When God takes us from bondage to liberty He puts words into our mouth and dancing in our feet.

Chapter 22

The Test of Continuing Faith
(Exodus 15:22–16:3)

The people of Israel were led away from the 'Reed Sea' (as it should be called) and were taken towards Mount Sinai (15:22). They go three days journey from the Reed Sea, to a place called the 'wilderness of Shur'.

From the start the Israelites had shown a strange mixture of faith and unbelief. Even at the very point when they were being redeemed they had criticised Moses (15:11) and had expected to die in the wilderness (15:11). They were speaking of dying in the wilderness even before they left Egypt (15:12)!

Now, for the second time, they show the unbelief which is mixed in with their faith. They came to Marah – the word means 'Bitterness'. It was called 'Marah' because the water there was so bitter in taste that it was undrinkable (15:23). For the second time they turn to grumbling and complaining. Again their grumbling is especially directed at Moses, the leader God has given to them (15:24).

This Israelite unbelief was a serious matter. It was a sin of ingratitude. One would expect them to be joyful and triumphant. They had seen the utter destruction of Pharaoh; he had been totally removed from ever bothering them again. They were failing to learn from what God had done. If He had delivered them in such a mighty way at the crossing of the Reed Sea, could God not do a similar work on their behalf to rescue them?

Moses' response to their criticism is to do nothing but pray (15:25a). God answered him as he was interceding for His people. Moses was shown a tree and was led to throw the tree into the large pool at Marah. The pool became sweet, and the people were able to drink the water.

Exodus 15:25b explains the significance of what had happened: 'there he tested them'. After we have experienced redemption God may test us to find out – and let us ourselves find out – whether we shall continue to believe, despite the practical problems that might confront us. The God who saves us also meets our needs as He continues to lead and guide us. If God had wonderfully rescued them from Egypt, the rest of His promises would be fulfilled as well. He had said He would take them to Mount Sinai (Exodus 3:12). God would certainly keep His promise. There was no need for the grumbling. The answer would have come **without their having to grumble and complain**. They were being tested. Could they face an alarming situation and yet continue to trust God so that they would not turn to grumbling and the criticism of their God-given leader?

They have been rescued from the angel of death, rescued from the wrath of Pharaoh, now they are rescued from the threat of fatal thirst at Marah. The sweetening of the waters enables them to meet their need of water, and little further along the way they come to Elim where there was an abundance of refreshment. At that place there were twelve springs and seventy date palms. They were able to rest at that spot and be abundantly refreshed. Their complaining was unnecessary.

What had happened at Marah was intended to be a permanent lesson for the Israelites. God made for them a 'statute', a permanent principle. He was letting them see by a practical experience that their ingratitude and complaining and criticism of Moses was all entirely unnecessary. God makes them an offer. If they will obey God, He will keep them free from the diseases of the Egyptians. It is not a promise that no sickness at all will ever come to them, but the kind of sicknesses that troubled the Egyptians will not trouble them. It is the very character of God to heal; His name is '**Yahweh Rapha**', 'the Lord who heals'.

Yet despite God's renewing the people, soon they fall into similar unbelief yet again. The people leave Elim and come to the wilderness of Zin (16:1; it has nothing to do with the English word 'sin'!) They have been travelling for about five weeks (see 15:3; 16:1) and now again they start bitterly complaining against Moses. It involves a rejection of Moses' call. Although it should have been perfectly plain that it was God who had brought them to where they were, they talk as if it is entirely Moses' doing ('**you** have brought us out into this wilderness', 16:3). Again they panic. Again they grumble. Again they attack Moses. Now they glamorise the past and talk as if Egypt were a wonderful place! 'We sat by pots of meat ... we ate bread to the full', (15:3). They were not thinking of days when they sighed because of their bondage and cried out to God for help (see 2:23). Apparently they now regarded Egypt as a good place to be! There are four lessons we must learn.

1. **Saving faith must become practical faith**. The people were saved by their faith in the blood of the lamb. But now their faith must face practical problems as they travel towards Sinai.

2. **It is only a matter of time before something tests our practical faith**. Five weeks after their salvation, the tests began! God came to them and said in effect: 'you believed before but will you believe now? You had faith enough to be saved by the blood of the lamb. Will you have faith enough to face these daily difficulties?'

3. **The test of faith consists in the seeming absence of God**. At first when the troubles came God did not seem to be there. He was not doing anything. He was waiting. God sometimes seems to hide himself for a while.

4. **God wants us to learn not to grumble against Him**. When we are in a crisis we are under test. We are faced with the temptation to lapse into self-pity. We are likely to be looking backwards and to be glamorising the past. But God does not like it. His ways with us are always good and 'in the time of need' He will rescue us in His own way.

Chapter 23

Manna from Heaven

(Exodus 16:4–36)

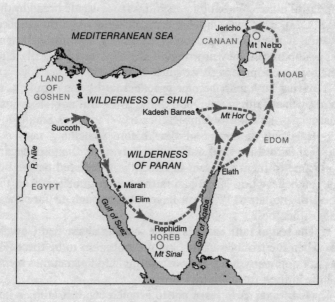

The people have left the Sea of Reeds (15:22) and have travelled into the wilderness of Shur (15:22). They have passed Marah (15:23) and Elim (15:27) and are now in the wilderness of Zin (16:1) where again they are complaining in unbelief (16:3). They are facing the trials and the testings of faith. They have shown faith in crossing the Reed Sea (see Hebrews 11:29). Now will they apply their faith when they meet practical difficulties? First they faced the enmity of Pharaoh – but God destroyed Pharaoh and he is no longer around to trouble them. Then they lacked water and God gave it to them. Now they have no food (16:3). They have twice had opportunities to learn that God will continue to meet their needs. The God who saved them by the blood of the lamb will continue to care for them. But will they trust Him?

Immediately it becomes clear that their grumbling is needless. Every time the people of Israel groan and complain they are very close to their rescue. When they complained about Pharaoh and his armies, he was about to be destroyed so that 'not even one of them remained' (Exodus 14:28). When they complained about there being no water at Marah, the water was just about to be purified for them (Exodus 15:25). Whenever they complain the remedy is near at hand. So it is again when they grumble about having no food while in the wilderness of Zin. God is just about to literally drop food for them from the sky (Exodus 16:4). God was about to provide for them. They were grumbling but God was already announcing what He was about to do.

So God sent the manna. The Hebrew word ('manna') seems to be a very old word meaning 'What is it?' They called the food the 'what-is-it', the 'what's-its-name', the 'manna'.

The manna tested their obedience. They had to collect it each day. They could not store it. It had to be collected one day at a time. If they tried to store it, it would go bad and could not be used. But there was an exception for the Sabbath (16:5). On Friday God would send twice as much and they would not have to collect manna on Saturday, the Sabbath! The people were approaching Sinai. Soon the law about the sabbath would be given. God was getting them ready for the Sabbath-law which had never been in existence before this time.

The manna demonstrated that their ultimate leader was God. They were always criticising Moses. But their leader was God. He was the one who was providing for them. Moses was the one appointed by God, but Moses had not brought them out of Egypt and Moses could not get food to fall from heaven. 'You will know that Yahweh has brought you out of the land of Egypt', said Moses. 'What are we that you grumble against us?' (16:6–7). Jesus made the same point; He obviously had studied this passage. 'It is not Moses who has given you the bread out of heaven, but it is My Father who gives you the true bread out of heaven...' (John 6:33).

If we attack one of God's leaders because we ourselves are full of unbelief, then we are attacking God. *'Your grumblings are ... against God'* (16:8).

The manna was proof of God's great care for His people. Even though the people grumbled against God, He still provided for them. Soon the glory of God appeared (16:9–10) and the people were promised meat in the morning and bread in the evening (16:11–12). Quails fell in the evening time (16:13) and the 'What-is-it', the manna, appeared in the morning (16:14–15).

However the people still were disobedient. They were told to collect just what they needed and that is what they did (16:16–18), but then they became disobedient. Some tried to leave some of the manna to be collected the next day (16:19–20). The manna fell in such a way that they did not have to collect it on the sabbath (16:21–26) but some of the people tried to collect it on the sabbath (16:27). Despite God's great care for them, they were still showing unbelief and disobedience (16:28–30).

It was called 'manna' (16:31) and later a pot of it was kept 'before the Lord' (that is, in the tabernacle when it was built) to remind them of how God provided for them (16:32–34). The manna continued to fall all the years they were in the wilderness. As soon as they crossed into Canaan forty years later, it ceased (16:35–36).

God meets our needs. His provision will fall day by day as we need it. He will never fail us. For the Christian the manna that comes from heaven is Jesus! Jesus said 'The bread of God is that which comes down out of heaven and gives life to the world' (John 6:33). Jesus came from heaven. His coming was entirely miraculous. 'I am the bread of life', said Jesus (John 6:35). 'The person who comes to me will never hunger, and the person who believes in me will never thirst' (John 6:35). We are to learn to live on Jesus as the Israelites lived on the manna. God gave them manna from heaven day after day regularly, persistently, unfailingly, all of their years in the wilderness. God will do the same to us. God will let Jesus be our food. Through Jesus God will give us strength and provision every day of our lives. When we need a double portion of strength He will give it to us.

We have to go to collect our manna every day. If we eat of Jesus every day, we shall never hunger. If we believe in Him daily, we shall never thirst.

Chapter 24

Massah and Meribah
(Exodus 17:1–7)

There now comes yet another story of the grumbling of Israel. It is the fourth (or the third since they left Egypt). First, they faced the enmity of Pharaoh. Then they lacked water at Marah (Exodus 15). Then they lacked food while in the wilderness of Zin (Exodus 16). Now there is a fourth incident that is similar. The people come to a place called Rephidim. It was a place where you would expect water because there was a spring there. But the spring had dried up and once again the people grumble. Again they criticise Moses (17:2). Moses reprimands them of putting Yahweh to the test. Do they not remember what happened before? Again Moses cries to God to rescue them in their need (17:4). Again God sends an answer (17:5–7). He takes the elders of the people so that the elders can witness what is happening and can learn a lesson for the future. He comes to a rock at Horeb.

This kind of event has now happened several times. One might expect that Israel would 'learn God's ways' (see the phrase in Hebrews 3:10). Some lessons ought now to have been learned by them.

1. **Faith gets tested**. They had exercised faith when they had trusted in the blood of the lamb. Every one of these Israelites were in families where the firstborn son, the leader of the family, had taken shelter under the blood of the lamb. Yet the question was: would they continue in faith? Would they hold to the faith they had professed earlier? Would they apply their faith in the daily difficulties they met along the way to the promised land?

2. **Saving faith must become diligent faith**. The faith that saved them must now be applied to their daily problems.

3. **What tests faith is a situation where God delays**. In each of these crises that they faced, God was ready with an answer to their need, but He came slower than they wanted, slower than they expected. There were times when they were in trouble yet God seemed to be absent. Faith believes that God is there (see Hebrews 11:6) even when He seems slow in coming.

The Israelites had now been through testing situations at least three or four times before. God was giving them many opportunities to learn. He was renewing them again unto repentance many times.

1. **They were grumbling against the guidance of God**. The people were travelling 'by stages from the wilderness of Zin, according to the command of Yahweh'. The pillar of cloud and pillar of fire was leading them. The trouble into which they came was trouble into which they were led by God. This is important. There is trouble into which we get ourselves by our own foolishness. But it is an entirely different matter when following the very detailed guidance of God gets us into trouble. These Israelites were being tested while they were in the will of God. The situation was not out of control. Moses was not making any mistakes. God was taking them where He wanted, step by step. Their complaints were complaints against God's guidance.

2. **What troubles them is disappointment**. They were expecting to find water at Rephidim. It was near a 'wadi', a stream. So they were exceptionally disappointed to find there was no water there after all. Disappointment is sometimes hard to take. It may lead us into complaining against God.

3. **They grumble against their leader**. As often, Moses has to bear the complaint of the people. 'Give us water...', they say (17:2). 'Why have you brought us up from Egypt...?'. They are talking as if Moses is God. It is not Moses who gives water. It was not Moses who rescued the people from Egypt. When people are falling into unbelief, they talk as if the leaders are God, and their complaints against God are turned upon the ones God has given them. They do not want to treat leaders as

God when the leaders are telling them what to do, but they wish to treat them as God when they are in trouble.

4. **They fall into self-pity**. These people are 'unbelieving believers'. They have sufficient faith to put their trust in the blood of the lamb but now they are full of doubts. Unbelieving believers fall into self-pity and negativism. 'You are planning to kill us', they say to Moses (17:3). 'We are about to die'. They have forgotten that when they were complaining previously, their rescue was always near at hand. They were more gloomy than they needed to be. It led them into extreme hostility towards Moses (17:4).

Again God had everything in hand. Moses took the matter to God (17:4). He was told to go before the people, taking some elders with him. What was about to happen was to be seen by all the people. He was to take the same staff that he had used before (17:5). It was to be a reminder that the God who had rescued before could rescue again. Moses is to strike the rock and water will pour out of it. This is what happens. At the end of everything, God had provided for them (17:6), but they had failed God's test. The grumbling made no difference. God provided for them, as He would have done whether they had grumbled or not. But their grumbling was yet again an expression of unbelief. The place was named Massah and Meribah ('Testing' and 'Grumbling', 17:7).

Complaining against God is a serious matter. What happens to us when there is a serious delay in the way God is leading us? The Israelites grumbled against the providence of God, against the guidance of God, against the goodness of God, against the wisdom of God. They accused His leader of malice against them.

Yet it was wonderful that God still rescued them.

Chapter 25

The Amalekites

(Exodus 17:8–16)

The people of Israel had been redeemed by the blood of the lamb. Now some people will have a hatred of God's people and will wish to destroy them (as in Exodus 17:8–16). But others wish to join the people of God (as in the next passage, Exodus 18:1–27). Some respond with hostility. Others are converted.

First comes aggression. The Amalekites initiate an attack upon the people of God (17:8). It was a painful experience for Israel. They were weary (see Deuteronomy 25:18) and the Amalekites descended from Abraham and Isaac. It is always painful when people you might expect to be your supporters become your enemies. It requires a very cool spirit and a strong determination not to be bitter at such a time.

1. **Moses faces the new enemy with a mixture of prayer and practicality**. First of all he does what the situation requires. Israel have no choice but to defend themselves. Joshua – who is mentioned here for the first time – must choose suitable men and must go out to do battle with the Amalekites (17:9a).

Moses himself will take 'the staff of God'. He will go to the top of the hill and there he will hold the staff up before God (17:9b). It is clear that this is some kind of praying. The word 'pray' is not used but it is clear that this is what is happening. The staff is the same one that had been used many times before. It had been in Moses' hands when at God's first interview with Moses God said 'What is in your hand?' (see 4:2).

Now he holds it up before God. It is as if he is saying 'Lord this is the sign that I am the person you chose for this work. I was carrying this staff when you called me. I held out this staff when we crossed the Reed Sea. You used this staff in connection with many wonderful answers to our need. Now, Lord, do it again!'

The important thing to notice is that **two things are happening here**. This conflict involves both practicality and prayer, fighting and faith. Some Christians are happy to take practical action when they are in trouble but they neglect to pray. Others want to pray but they do nothing practical. But it would have done no good to have Moses praying on the hill if there had been no Joshua fighting in the valley.

2. **The battle and the praying both require persistence**. Joshua begins to fight the Amalekites; Moses, Aaron and Hur are praying before God on the mountain top (17:10). Both the people in the valley and the people on the mountain soon discover that what they are doing will require persistence. The battle will go on a long time. As soon as Moses' praying begins to weaken the fighting begins to fail.

Praying requires persistence. 'People ought always to pray and not grow weary' (Luke 18:1).

3. **Our praying may need help**. Moses begins to weary in his position as intercessor. The spirit is willing but his flesh is weak. Like the three disciples praying late at night in the garden at Gethsemane (Matthew 26:36–45) he finds his physical tiredness overwhelms him. When he ceased to pray the battle began to go against the Israelites (17:11). So Moses' assistants help him. They enable him to sit and they support his hands (17:12). Moses stays in that posture until the victory is won (17:13). Although Joshua and Hur are not literally praying, their actions represent a kind of prayer. It is as if they are identifying with Moses' plea for God's help.

Intercession is hard work! No one need feel ashamed to find himself wearying in intercession. The flesh – the physical frame – is weak. Our bodies have weakness in them and the weakness of our physical nature affects us spiritually. But it helps if others come to aid and encourage us in intercession. It is easier to persist if others are with us.

4. **The battle will be sustained**. The people are warned that what has happened is not an isolated occurrence. It will occur

again, The story is recorded. 'Write it in the book,' says Moses.
Here is the origin of our first five books of the Bible. In the
Hebrew it speaks of 'the' book not 'a book'. Evidently there is
already a record being kept of what had been happening (see
also Exodus 24:4, 7; 34:27; Numbers 33:1–2; Deuteronomy
31:9, 11). Our book of Exodus may have been edited at a later
stage, but the process of writing it was started by Moses.

The record of the incident must be kept because the
Amalekites will continue to be a problem to Israel, yet they
must be utterly exterminated. Total extermination will be the
ultimate penalty for the Amalekites' rebellion against God
and their hatred of His people.[1] The Israelites must never
compromise with those who wish to wipe them out of existence.
Rather they are called to wipe the Amalekites out of existence.
The Amalekites' hatred of Israel would continue (Numbers
24:20; Deuteronomy 25:17–19; Joshua 2:9–11; 1 Samuel 15:18).
Even Haman who tried to annihilate Israel descended from
Agag, an Amalekite (see 1 Samuel 15:32; Esther 3:1). He was an
Amalekite trying to annihilate Israel, whereas Israel had been
commanded to annihilate the Amalekites.

The never-ending conflict between Israel and Amalek speaks
of the never-ending conflict between the church and the world,
between righteousness and sin. The battle will go on for a long
time. Eventually 'Amalek' will be exterminated. Meanwhile the
people of God must be ready for conflict.

There is one encouragement. Moses built an altar to remind
everyone that the battle had been won by the Lord. He names
the altar 'Yahweh Nissi', 'the Lord is my banner'. It was a
reminder that the people had been able to see Moses' praying.
He was like a banner held high for everyone to see. Similarly in
days of future conflict Yahweh would be their banner, the One
they looked to, to give them victory. God takes an oath (17:16).
'Yahweh has sworn by his kingship'[2] (17:16). Israel, whether as
an ancient nation or as today's people of God, will always have
to fight the world and its wickedness until the day comes when
wickedness is finally exterminated.

The Christian can see Jesus here. He ever lives to make
intercession until the battle is won.

Notes

[1] The Hebrew word is *machah*; it always and invariably means 'wipe out', 'blot out', 'utterly destroy'. It was used of the punishment at the time of the flood (Genesis 6:7; 7:4, 23), of having one's name or memory blotted out (Exodus 17:14; 32:32, 33; Deuteronomy 25:6, 19; 29:20; Psalm 9:5; 69:28; 109:13), of the blotting out of sins in total forgiveness (Nehemiah 4:5; Psalm 51:1, 9; 109:14; Isaiah 43:25; 44:22; Jeremiah 18:23) or blotting out in total forgetfulness of actions that have taken place (Nehemiah 13:14; Proverbs 6:33; Ezekiel 6:6), of wiping away curses so that they no longer exist (Numbers 5:23), of wiping a people out of existence (Deuteronomy 9:14; Judges 21:17; 2 Kings 14:27). And it can be used of wiping a dish clean so that no dirt is left (2 Kings 21:13) or wiping the mouth clean of food (Proverbs 30:20) or ending the reign of a king (Proverbs 31:3) or of the total ending of disgrace (Isaiah 25:8). Total annihilation or extermination is always involved.

[2] The Hebrew is literally 'A hand is upon the throne of Yah'.

Chapter 26

The Conversion of Jethro
(Exodus 18:1–27)

The story at this point is considering how gentiles react to Israel's salvation. Now a different kind of reaction is told to us in the story of Jethro's visit to Moses.

Actually the story is told to us out of chronological order! It is a story taken from the time when the Israelites had arrived at Mount Sinai. This is related to us in Exodus 19:1–2, but in Exodus 18:5 the Israelites are at Mount Sinai already! The story comes from a time after their arrival at Sinai but has been brought forward to be presented to us at this point. The reason for the sequence of stories seems to be that the writer is presenting **two** gentile reactions to Israel's redemption. The story has been brought forward to be a contrast to that of the Amalekites' hostility. If some people reacted to Israel with hate, others will react with approval and will want what Israel has. It often happens this way. When we are discouraged by un-expected opposition, God sends a friend to support us. When the Israelites faced the unexpected aggression of the Amalekites it would not be long before they were given an encouraging convert in the person of Jethro, Moses' father-in-law.

1. **First, we see what led to Jethro's conversion**. He discovered what God had done for Moses. He had known Moses for years. Now he hears of the wonderful things God had done for Moses (18:1). Yahweh had brought the people out of Egypt. Moses had sent his wife home, presumably at the time of his dangerous visits to Pharaoh (18:2–4). Now the family hear of what has happened, and his family come to him including Jethro (18:5–6). Moses goes out to meet him and tells him the whole story (18:7–8). Jethro is delighted. He is not a pagan who opposes

God's people – like the Amalekites. Rather he is converted and fully accepts the message of what God has done.

There were two stages to Jethro's conversion. First he heard generally the good news of what had happened to Israel. This is often the start of the way people are saved. They get a general impression that there is something good about what God has done. The message rings out in a general way (see 1 Thessalonians 1:8).

The second stage is involves talking face-to-face. Moses is given the opportunity to talk person-to-person with Jethro. It is wonderful when we are allowed to talk in this way about what God has done in redeeming us.

2. **Next, we see what his conversion consisted of**. He came to faith in the God of Israel. At one stage it seems he had been the priest of a pagan religion. Now he knows that Israel's God is the one and only God. He hears that Yahweh – the God of Israel – has acted (18:1). He rejoices *'over all the good things that Yahweh had done for Israel'* (18:9). He accepts it heartily (18:10). He has come to a sure knowledge that Yahweh is greater than all rivals (18:11).

His salvation consists of faith in the blood of a lamb. He offers a burnt-offering speaking of total consecration to God (18:12). He offers a peace-offering which involved a meal. He has a peace-offering meal with the leaders of Israel; he is joining the people of God. These are the ingredients of true conversion.

3. **Next, we see what followed Jethro's conversion**. He immediately was given gifts of wisdom. He became a sensible and observant person. He sees Moses doing his work as the one-and-only judge of Israel. Cases come to Moses all day (18:13) and Jethro sees it (18:14a). Immediately he sees that what is happening lacks wisdom. He protests: 'Why do you alone sit as judge?' he asks (18:14b). Moses explains (18:15–16), and Jethro makes a suggestion.

God is concerned about the physical side to our work. Moses is only flesh-and-blood. There is a limit to how much physical strain we can take. Jethro sees this and instantly, as a new convert, but as a wise person, suggests that Moses gets helpers to assist him in his work. As the work of God grows the number of people in the work must multiply. God gave Moses prayer-partners in Rephidim (17:8–16). He gives Moses assistants at Sinai (18:13–27). A sensible servant of God will look after his body. He or she will see that they have enough sleep, enough rest, enough food. Jesus was concerned about these things during His ministry. 'Come apart and rest awhile', He could say to His disciples.

When God's work goes forward it involves delegation. Jethro puts it to Moses. 'What you are doing is not sensible', he says (18:17). Moses will wear himself out physically (18:18). 'You be for the people their organiser in the sight of God', Jethro says (18:19). Moses must teach the commands of God (18:20). When it comes to administering the commands and dealing with cases that arise he must have the help of judges who will work with a hierarchy of lesser courts (18:21–22). A meeting with Moses will be the final court of appeal. In this way Moses will stay healthy and the people's need will be met (18:23).

It is good advice, and Moses does as Jethro suggests (18:24–26). After that Jethro goes home (18:27). He was a man who became useful in God's work as soon as he came to faith. God's people are given gifts. The moment they come to salvation God has planted within them capacities that will contribute to His kingdom. Jethro instantly had a gift of wisdom, and used it straightaway in the kingdom of God.

Exodus 18 is jumping ahead in the story. The people of Israel arrived at Mount Sinai (19:1–2). God had fulfilled His word. This was the very place where Moses had taken his flocks to find pasture. It was on the slopes of Mount Sinai or Horeb that God had manifested Himself as a burning fire that needed no fuel. God had saved His people by the blood of the lamb. The flame of holiness that had appeared to Moses (3:2) had followed them all the way. Now God will enter into a covenant relationship with them. They have been saved by the blood of the lamb, but that has to be worked out in their lives and their future. They are saved for fellowship, saved for worship, saved to walk in obedience to God's commands. Fifty days after their redemption by the blood of the lamb God gave the people His law.

It is similar in pattern with the salvation of Jesus. Fifty days after the blood of Jesus was shed the Holy Spirit came down upon the disciples. We too are saved in order to walk by the Spirit and so fulfil the law of God given to Israel. We first experience passover: not an animal but a divine Saviour who has died for us. Then we are brought to our Sinai: not a mountain that may be touched and a blazing fire outside of us, but a Holy Spirit that is experienced and a fire blazing within us that we may fulfil the law of Christ.

Chapter 27

God Introduces His Covenant of Law

(Exodus 19:1–5a)

The story picks up from the last-mentioned location, Rephidim (see Exodus 17:1, 7). From Rephidim the Israelites travelled without any further stopping-places until they reached the uninhabited area around Mount Sinai. They arrived on the 'third new moon'. They had travelled from the 14th of the first month (12:6, 29), throughout the second month, and they arrived at the beginning of the third month, just under fifty days after the first and original passover. The Festival of Weeks (Exodus 34:22) or 'harvest festival' (23:16) or 'Day of Pentecost' (Acts 2:1) was kept fifty days after Passover (see Leviticus 23:16). Fifty days after Passover became the traditional time for the anniversary of the giving of the law.

Verse 2 gives further detail. *'They set out from Rephidim and came to the wasteland of Sinai and they settled their camp in the wasteland. There Israel had their camp near the mountain'* (19:2).

'The mountain' is Mount Sinai, also called Horeb. It is probably in the south of what is now called the Sinai peninsula. As soon as they arrived *'Moses went up to God'* (19:3). He walks uphill to the lower slopes of the mountain. It is the place where the burning bush had been (see Exodus 3:1–3), and where he had talked with God.

This is the next great lesson of the Bible: **salvation by the blood of the lamb is only the beginning of God's purpose for His people**. The newly redeemed people of God have been taken to Sinai. Redemption is with a view to worship. 'When you have brought the people out of Egypt you will worship God on this mountain', said God (3:12). God saves us with a view to getting our lives to be under His guidance. The blood of our Lord Jesus Christ was shed so that He might 'redeem us from all iniquity and purify for himself a people of His own who are zealous for good deeds' (Titus 2:14). In fifty days God took Israel from Passover to Sinai. In fifty days God took the church from the shedding of Jesus' blood to the outpouring of the Holy Spirit. God put Israel under His law. Applying Exodus 19–24 to ourselves, we shall see how God gives us the Spirit and we fulfil the law by walking in the Spirit. He takes us from Passover to Pentecost.

God is about to require that His people submit to a law-covenant. We shall learn some things about 'covenant' in this part of the Bible. *'God speaks: and Yahweh called to him from the from the mountain, "This is what you shall say to the family of Jacob, and tell the people of Israel ... "'* (19:3). A covenant is a relationship between people where promises are given and are confirmed by the taking of an oath. There were different kinds of 'covenant' in the ancient world. In earlier parts of the Bible we have had covenants of generosity, in connection with the stories of Noah and Abraham. And we have seen a mutual covenant in connection with Abraham and Abimelech. Now we come to a covenant of imposed-obligation or a covenant of law.

In a **covenant of generosity** the senior partner is being generous and he swears to convey some blessing or benefit upon the other partner in the covenant. God's covenants with Noah and Abraham were 'covenants of generosity'.

In a **mutual covenant**, both partners take an oath. There is no 'mutual' covenant with God. God is always the senior in the covenant relationship.

In a **covenant of law** the senior partner imposes his will on the junior partner and the junior partner has to take the oath. In this case the oath is an oath of loyalty or an oath promising obedience.

In Exodus chapters 19–24 we are seeing a covenant of law being imposed upon the people of Israel. However it is being imposed in a very kindly way and Israel is happy to swear obedience to God.

Moses is to take a message to the people. God wants to make a covenant of law with them. He wants a treaty in which God promises to be their God, and they swear to obey Him.

1. **The invitation to enter a covenant begins with a statement of God's generosity**. Often in ancient covenants the covenant-maker would begin with summarising what good things he had done for the junior partner in the covenant. God begins: *'You yourselves have seen what I did to the Egyptians, and how I carried you on eagles' wings, and brought you to myself'* (19:4). God had defeated their enemies and protected Israel in a powerful way. He had since met their every need as they had travelled to Sinai. Eagles were famous for protecting their young. God was protecting His people.

Although this is a 'covenant of law' there is a lot of generosity and kindness in it. The Bible contrasts law and grace (John 1:17; Romans 6:14) but even when God gave His law there was a lot of His graciousness in what He did! The Christian is under a different kind of covenant – the 'new covenant'. But every one of God's covenants begins with His generosity. In the ancient world eagles were famous for their strength, their beauty, their glory, their marvellous eyesight, their care of their young. God says to us: 'You have seen what I did to your old enemies, and how I carried you on eagles' wings, and brought you to myself'.

God is so merciful to us! He breaks the power of sin. He overcomes Satan and his powers. He overcomes the enemies of the Christian fellowship. He protects us, overshadowing us like an eagle spreads out her wings over her young. He carries us to where we need to be. He did that for Israel; He has done the same for us.

Above all He takes the initiative in bringing us to Himself. 'I carried you . . . I brought you to myself', said God to Israel, and He has done the same in the life of every Christian. Now He wants to introduce us to the life of obedience. In the case of Israel it was the life of obedience to the Mosaic law; with the Christian it is the life of obedience in the power of the Spirit. It is different, but it is parallel.

Chapter 28

The Promise of the Law

(Exodus 19:5b–8)

2. **The covenant via Moses had a condition attached to it**. This is not a covenant of sheer generosity (which also requires obedience but after God's oath is given it is unconditional). God is not the one taking an oath. It is not like the unconditional promise of Genesis 9:21 or Genesis 22:15–18. It is not that kind of covenant. From the very beginning there is a condition to be met before the blessings of the covenant will come (19:5).

Life in the Holy Spirit is not identical but it is parallel. It also has a condition attached to it. Israel was given its national redemption but there was a condition to experiencing God's fullness of blessing in their national life. Similarly, the Christian is given his or her redemption but there is a condition to experiencing God's kingdom in its fullness. Only **if** we sow to the Spirit shall we reap back from the Holy Spirit the full blessings of eternal life. **If** we mortify the deeds of the body, we shall live. **If** we keep coming to Jesus and keep drinking from Him, we shall experience His 'rivers of the living water'.

3. **The covenant has promises attached to it**. If they will obey their divine King, He will bring three things about in their lives. (i) They will be God's special treasure. *'Now therefore if you will listen ... if you will keep my commandment, then you will be my own special treasure among all the peoples, for all the earth is mine'* (19:5).

(ii) The entire nation will be a nation of priests. *'... and you shall be a kingdom of priests ... '*.

And (iii) the nation will be a nation specially consecrated to God: *'... a kingdom of priests and a holy nation'* (19:6a).

Moses had to put this matter to Israel (19:6b). Moses then takes the message back (19:7). The people respond to what God has said. *'Everything that Yahweh has said we shall do'* (19:8a). This leads to Moses' going for the third time some distance up the lower slopes of the mountain (19:8b).

So far, what is happening is simply preliminary. The covenant demands have to be given; we have them in Exodus 20:1–23:19). Then the actual covenant will have to be made by the people's giving their oath (Exodus 24:3). At present Yahweh is simply telling the people through Moses what will be involved.

The obedient people of God are His 'special possession'. The word 'special possession' was used in the ancient world to speak of a king's private money. If Christians will obey God's Spirit, God will treasure them. They will reap back rich spiritual experience from the Holy Spirit. The Christian will belong to God and be honoured by God. God is the Lord of the entire earth, but He will relate very personally and intimately to that one who gives heed to the voice of the Holy Spirit.

God will prize such people. They will be used by God. He will use them to further His purpose; no other people will be used in such a way. They will be protected by Yahweh, cared for by Yahweh – just as a king guards his personal treasure.

The obedient people of God are a 'kingdom of priests'. The promise was held out for Israel. It refers not just to the tribe of Levi but to the whole nation. The entire nation would have a priestly function towards the world. In Israel, priests gave sacrificial offerings and interceded with God; they were the teachers of the people. If Israel will be obedient they will be intercessors for the world and will be teachers of the world.

The obedient Christian inherits the promise. His or her obedience to the Holy Spirit results in God's being attentive to his intercessions. Because they obey God, all God's obedient people become 'a kingdom of priests'. They intercede and God hears their prayers. They find that they are able to minister to others. God uses them as the teachers of His word, not in a professional manner but simply as those who are being honoured by God. They have something to say and they say it with conviction and with authority.

This is an unusual promise. Obedience to the law would lead to the royal priesthood of all Israelites. It never really happened because the Israelites never were very obedient to the law. The offer is held out to the Christian at a higher level. For those obedient to the voice of the Spirit the 'priesthood of all believers' will take powerful effect in their lives.

The obedient people of God are a 'holy nation'. Israel, if obedient to the law, would stand out in distinctiveness and uniqueness among the nations of the world. In the event, Israel gradually lost its distinctiveness and became like the other nations. At times they were even consciously ambitious to be like the other nations. Yet God was offering them uniqueness and distinctiveness. Again the church inherits the promise at a higher level. 'You are a chosen race, a royal priesthood, a holy nation, a people for God's own possession', said Peter to his people scattered through the Roman provinces around the east end of the Mediterranean Sea (1 Peter 2:9; 1:1).

4. **The covenant has a mediator in it.** God is not speaking to the people directly. He is speaking through Moses. Equally the people are not speaking to God directly. They are speaking through Moses as well. Moses is a two-way mediator.

This too is different but parallel in the case of the gospel of Jesus. It is different in that the mediator is Jesus. It is parallel in that there is no contact with God except through Jesus. God does not speak to us except through Jesus, and we cannot speak to God except through Jesus. 'No person comes to the Father except through me', He said (John 14:6).

Chapter 29

Getting Ready to Meet God
(Exodus 19:9–15)

Moses reported the words of the people to Yahweh (19:8b). This is Moses' third meeting with God on Sinai (19:8b–15). The people are happy to be in relationship with God as their Master and King.

Now God appears to Moses in a thick cloud (19:9a). God's shining glory will be within the cloud, so as not to be seen. God will speak audibly from the lower slopes of Sinai and the people will be able to hear what God says. This will give them overwhelming evidence that Moses is the supreme mediator between God and Israel. They relate to God via Moses, and in no other way. They must put their trust in Moses in order to be in touch indirectly with God. Again this is 'parallel but distinct' when applied to Jesus. Moses is a 'type', a foreshadowing of Jesus. The Christian has Jesus alone as his or her mediator. We relate to God via Jesus, and in no other way. We must put our trust in Jesus in order to be in touch with God through Him.

Moses relays to God the people's answer (19:9b). God gives instructions (19:10–11). The people must be spiritually prepared for a 'theophany' – a visible representation of God. The washed clothes speak of a clean life. Clothes are what we see when we look at another person. So clothing stands for the person's character and reputation as we look at him. (This is why we need to be 'clothed' with the righteousness of Jesus Christ.)

The people must not come too near the place where God is revealing himself to Moses. A boundary is to be marked out over which the people must not come (19:12–13a).

A semi-circular border must be made. Moses is allowed up the lower slopes of the mountain but the people are not! They must not have any physical contact at all with the lower slopes of the mountain. If they do the death penalty will follow.

These requirements let us know something of the nature of the covenant that is about to come into being. It is a revelation of fearful holiness. It has in it requirements that are to be kept, out of fear of punishment. From its earliest mention fear of punishment is involved in the law. The Mosaic covenant creates distance between man and God. It did not bring people near; it kept them away. There was however a point where they would be invited to go somewhat nearer to where God was revealing Himself on the lower slopes of Sinai. The lengthy trumpet blast would reveal the time for the move nearer to the place where God was speaking. *'When the trumpet sounds in a drawn-out signal, they shall come up to the mountain'* (19:13b).

Moses returns to the people and passes on these instructions. *'And Moses went down from the mountain to the people. He sanctified the people and they washed their clothes. And he said to the people, "Be ready for the third day. Do not approach a woman"'* (19:14–15). They wash their clothes – a ceremony that speaks of cleansing one's life (19:14). They are to abstain from sexual pleasures (19:15), not because they are wrong but because there are times in life when earthly pleasures must be left aside temporarily in order to concentrate on relating to God.

Several principles stand out in the story at this point.

1. **We note the fearful holiness of God**. He cannot be seen. A thick cloud has to cover even His partial appearing. One look at the shining holiness of God would kill any sinful human being who seeks to approach God.

2. **The servants of God need authentication**. One reason why there is much display and ceremony in this story is so that the people may believe Moses (see 19:9). Who is Moses that he should take this authoritative and unsurpassed role in governing Israel and its relationship to God. He needs heavenly authentication of some kind.

3. **Relationship with God requires a Mediator**. God cannot be approached directly. His burning holiness makes Him in a sense unapproachable. Yet God wants to be approached and wants

to have dealings with men and women. How can it be done? God's way is to appoint a Go-Between, a Mediator.

4. **Relationship with God requires preparation**. We shall do well when we seek to meet with God to prepare ourselves. Under the gospel it will not be clothes that have to be cleaned but character. The clothes were the symbol; character is the reality. If we regard sin in our hearts God will take no notice of us (Psalm 66:18). Sometimes even the ordinary joys of life must be left aside for a while in order that we might concentrate on God.

5. But of course **there is much in this story that calls not for comparison but for contrast**. Hebrews 12:18 was expounding by way of contrast more than by way of comparison, when it said: *'You have not come to a mountain that might be touched ... '*. The message of Sinai was: come towards the mountain but do not come too close. The message of the blood of Jesus Christ is: come as close as you possibly can! Draw near with confidence (Hebrews 4:16)! When we read the law we must do some contrasting as well as some comparing. *'Let us draw near with a sincere heart in full assurance of faith, having our hearts sprinkled clean from an evil conscience ... '* (Hebrews 10:22).

We too are waiting for a trumpet-blast. Again God will descend to meet us. 'The Lord himself will descend from heaven ... with the trumpet of God' (1 Thessalonians 4:16). We wait for a trumpet blast, but when it comes we shall be taken as near as near can be, 'for ever with the Lord' (1 Thessalonians 4:17).

Chapter 30

The Appearing of God's Glory
(Exodus 19:16–25)

On the third morning God appears (19:16a). There is thunder, lightning, and thick cloud. It is the appearing of God's glory. Thunder was the loudest sound heard by the ancient world. Lightning was the most dramatic flash of light. The loudest sound and the most dramatic flash of light together represent the glory of God's burningly pure, sin-hating nature. The cloud obscures and covers the glory and lets us know that God cannot be totally and directly observed. His glory has to be partly concealed by the cloud; human nature is unable bear the totally displayed radiation of God's nature. This is a common theme in connection with the glory of God.

A trumpet-sound, like that of a ram's horn but louder, signals the coming of God. It sounds out so loudly that the people are afraid (19:16b). They are led to the lower slopes of Mount Sinai (19:17). It is taken for granted that they do not go over the limits mentioned in verse 12. The way for God's coming has been prepared. Everyone knows what is to happen. The smoke now encircles the entire mountain; the whole mountain is a vibrating furnace (19:18). The fire of the burning bush (3:1–4:17) which became a pillar of fire (13:21–22), has now become a burning mountain. God comes down and thick smoke went up like smoke from a furnace. The smoke also speaks of God's power to destroy, as rubbish is burnt in a furnace. Abraham had seen something similar. When Sodom was exterminated by the fire of God, Abraham saw the 'dense smoke ... like the smoke from a furnace' (Genesis 19:28). The trumpet sound gets louder and louder (19:19a).

Verse 19b says 'Moses was speaking and God kept answering him in a loud voice'. We are not told what they were saying to each other; the uniqueness of Moses as a mediator between God and the people is being emphasised.

God comes from such a great height that He has to descend to reach the top of the mountain (compare Genesis 11:4, 5 where the top of the tower of Babel is in the sky, but God has to come down to see it!) The descent has already been mentioned (19:18). The style of the description is detailed and repetitive; vital events are generally told in a very repetitive manner in Hebrew narrative. Moses is summoned to come to the top of the mountain. It is his fourth ascent recorded in the book of Exodus. The previous three occasions involved Moses going some distance up the lower slopes (3:1–3; 19:3; 8b). Now for the first time Moses is called to a higher level where God will speak to him (19:20) but as soon as he ascends to this point he is sent down again to warn the people not to break through the barrier that has been marked out (19:21; see 19:12). Even the priests who can come partway up the mountain may not come as far as Moses comes and must specially consecrate themselves ready for the approach towards God (19:22). No priests have been mentioned before! It is likely that already the tribe of Levi is beginning to do priestly duty. They must take special care. Moses seems to think that to warn the people again is unnecessary (19:23) but God insists. He tells Moses that, when he ascends the mountain again, he must return with Aaron (19:24–25).

As the chapter closes (in our English Bibles) Moses is with the people; he is still with them at the end of the giving of the Ten Commandments (in 20:18–20). Only after the giving of the ten commands does he ascend to God again (see 20:21). Although Moses is God's mediator, he is as much under the law as anyone else. 'Moses was faithful as a servant' (Hebrews 3:5). He was not exempt from the law himself. Nor was Jesus. Although He was faithful as a Son (Hebrews 3:6), He still was born under the Mosaic law (Galatians 4:4).

A number of points are specially worth noting.

1. **The law is truly from God**. This can scarcely be doubted but is worthy of special mention because the Bible comes to a

negative conclusion concerning the law. Jeremiah will point out its failure. A new covenant will be needed, 'It will not be like the covenant that I made ... a covenant that they broke...' (Jeremiah 31:32). Yet the law 'came with glory' (2 Corinthians 3:7). However provisional and inadequate it may turn out to be, it nevertheless came from God, and came with a revelation of the glory of God's nature. Yet it was only temporary. Paul makes the point that the 'ministry of the Spirit' comes in even greater glory (2 Corinthians 3:8). And when the ministry of the Spirit comes – says Paul – the glory of the law is set aside because the coming of the Spirit has displaced the law (2 Corinthians 3:9–11). Yet the law was never evil, never demonic. It was always 'holy, righteous and good' (Romans 7:12). It was the people who failed, not the law ('a covenant that **they** broke', Jeremiah 31:32).

2. **The law revealed God's sin-hating purity and majestic power**. The law came with a revelation of God's glory that aroused fear and terror. God's nature was revealed as burningly holy, and full of bright illumination. The shaking of an entire mountain – and mountains were famous for being inflexibly stationary – showed the greatness of God's power. When holy hatred of sin is allied to majestic mountain-shaking power we have a revelation of God's nature that is stunning and fearful.

3. **The law arouses only fear**. There is nothing in this revelation of God that can arouse anything but deep fear in the people. *'All the people ... trembled'* (19:16). The law would restrain sin out of fear, but it would never arouse affection or love of God. This eventually would turn out to be its greatest weakness. Fear never arouses love, and yet the heart of righteousness is love. The law did not draw people towards God; it drove them away from God. God knew what He was doing when He gave His people the law, but it was only a temporary measure. It would have the effect of preserving the nation of Israel, and by preserving the nation of Israel it would prepare for the coming of Jesus. The law is not against the promises of God already given to Abraham. Yet it will take something more than the revelation of God's holiness to bring men and women to true righteousness of heart. The law will prove to be a

ministry of death. 'If there was glory in the ministry which imparts condemnation, much more does the ministry which gives us righteousness abound in glory! Indeed, what once had glory has lost its glory because of the greater glory'. The law was bad news for sinners. It came with the brightness of God's glory. The law was temporary; something permanent has come in Jesus. 'What was set aside came accompanied with glory' but now 'much more has the permanent come in glory!' (see 2 Corinthians 3:7–11). The law had fading glory; the good news of Jesus has permanent glory.

Chapter 31

The Ten Commandments

(Exodus 20:1–6)

At Exodus 20:1, Moses is among the people. At this point the law is being announced to Moses as well as to the people. Although he has been the mediator through whom God has spoken to the people, the law is for him as well for everyone else.

Now God speaks (20:1). *'I am Yahweh your God, who brought you out of the land of Egypt, out of the house of slavery . . .'* (20:2). Before the 'ten words' of Exodus 20:3–17 are given, God tells of how He has redeemed the people from bondage. Obedience to God's commands will express gratitude for what God has already done. The reason why God saved them was not because they were law-abiding. God saved them from Egypt without any law at all, but now He wishes to give His redeemed people His law. It is a common pattern throughout the Bible. After having been brought to salvation, God wants our obedience.

We come now to **the first commandment**: *'You shall have no other gods before me'* (Exodus 20:3). Maybe other nations will worship their so-called gods, but Israel is not to tolerate any other so-called 'god' in the presence of Yahweh. Maybe there are people in Israel who are not very clear that other gods are nonentities, but the law of God is clear. No other god is to be allowed in Israel. All over the land of Israel, where the Israelites will live and where Yahweh will be specially present, idolatry of any kind is to be severely forbidden.

The 'you' in this command is addressed to the individual. The Hebrew language has a plural 'You' and a singular 'You', and the word here is singular 'You as an individual shall have no other gods before me'. This is rather striking since the law is obviously being given to a nation. Yet although the entire nation are present at the foot of Mount Sinai, each individual Israelite is to hear God as though God were speaking to him or her alone. The same thing was true on the Day of Pentecost which was the anniversary of the giving of the law. The Spirit came down upon them as they were 'all together', but the Spirit also rested on 'each one of them' (Acts 2:1, 3). The giving of the law was both corporate and personal; so was the giving of the Spirit which would enable the fulfilling of the law.

The first command meant that the Israelite and anyone living among them was literally not allowed to profess faith in or worship or acknowledge any other god. If anyone sacrificed to any god other than Yahweh he was executed (Exodus 22:20).

'You shall have no other gods before me', said the first commandment. No, of course not! The Christian hardly needs to be told. The works of the flesh are plain!

It means that we deny the reality of any other god. We refuse every kind of idol, especially the idolatry of money. We do not turn religion into business. We refuse the idolatry of self. We refuse the idolatry of self-trust and lukewarmness in the things of God.

But the Christian will fulfil the command positively as well as negatively. Led by the Holy Spirit, he or she will openly acknowledge that the God of the Bible is the one and only God, the one he or she worships. The Holy Spirit will lead us in this way.

The Christian also fulfils **the second commandment** by walking in the Spirit. *'You shall not make for yourself an image or any likeness of any creature in the heavens above or on the earth or in the waters which are lower than the earth'* (Exodus 20:4). In the heavens – the sky – there are the sun and moon and the stars. On earth there are people and animals. In the sea, that is, the waters that are lower than the earth, there are fish and sea creatures of various kinds. In the ancient world gods were made from images taken from all three realms. At one stage the Egyptians worshipped the sun. At Ur where Abraham originated, they worshipped the moon. Others worshipped the stars. Different people worshipped different animals. Others worshipped gods that were modelled on creatures from the sea. The use of 'images' like these were forbidden to the Israelites. *'You shall not bow down to them, and you shall not worship them'* (20:5a).

Why is it wrong to use an image to worship God? One reason is that God cannot be easily represented by a dead and cold picture or statue. Often when God appeared there would be no form visible at all. 'You saw no form on the day when Yahweh spoke to you at Horeb...', said Moses later (Deuteronomy 4:15–18). The reason Moses gave for God's not letting the people see a shape was 'lest you act corruptly by making a graven image ... in the form of any figure...'.

When you use an idol to represent God you invariably start talking to the idol. You address the image in prayer. God can only become visibly accessible when He takes the initiative to 'appear' and when He does so He also speaks. He appears as the God who talks. This is one of the differences between God and the idols. 'The idols ... cannot speak', said Jeremiah (Jeremiah 10:5). Images are not to be used. God will not tolerate false representation.

God explains why He cannot tolerate an idol. *'For I, Yahweh your God, am a jealous God, punishing the iniquity of fathers on children, upon the third and fourth generation of them that hate me* (20:5b), *but showing kindness to thousands of generations, for those who love me and keep my commands'* (20:6). God is a 'jealous' God. He cannot tolerate a rival.

Chapter 32

The Third and Fourth Commandments
(Exodus 20:7–11)

The **third commandment** refers to the way in which we think and talk about God. God had revealed His name, Yahweh, to Israel. He made known His holy character. He revealed Himself as the God who redeems by the blood of the lamb. The point of the third commandment was to protect the holy character of God. No one in Israel was allowed to start casually speaking of Yahweh with no special purpose in his talk. It would give a false impression of Yahweh, the God who had redeemed the people by the blood of the passover lamb.

Negatively, the third command meant that one was not to use God's name casually. The name 'Yahweh' (sometimes spelled Jehovah but mistakenly) was not to be used carelessly; it was the name to which God gave meaning at the time of the exodus. One's general references to God were not to be so casual as to slander His holy character.

In Israel the third command meant that one would never use the name 'Yahweh' of a false god (as the Israelites would soon do when they worshipped Yahweh in the form of a golden calf). It meant that they were not to use talk about God to get their own will done. They were not to try to manipulate people by using God's name when putting pressure on them. They were not to abuse the name Yahweh when taking vows or oaths.

The command meant that they were to let God be Himself! They were to honour Yahweh as the God who redeemed them. They were to praise Him and worship Him as He really is. They were to call upon Him in time of trouble, and ask His blessing over everything they did. They were to speak of His name to the surrounding nations, pointing the peoples of the world to the one-and-only Yahweh who had saved Israel and who intended to bring world-wide blessing through Israel, The third command would be upheld by punishment for any who misused the name 'Yahweh'.

The 'name' of God is His radiating, active, shining presence and power. To revere the 'name' of God was a matter of very great importance in ancient Israel, and in their own way Christians fulfil the third command.

The **fourth command** concerns 'the sabbath day'. The sabbath was first of all an event in the life of God. The command has its background in creation, as Exodus 20:11 says. God is like a workman. He did the work of creating the universe in six 'days', and then on a seventh 'day' (which has still not ended) He rested. God's sabbath is His enjoyment of what He had done. It included God's desire to share what He had done. He wished to involve the human race in His enjoyment.

So important was this 'sabbath-rest' of God, it became part of the 'Ten Commandments', the central ten-point summary of everything that God was wanting His people Israel to do. It was extraordinarily important and the breaking of the sabbath brought upon itself the death penalty.

Jesus honoured the Saturday-sabbath but resisted enlargements of it and prepared the way for its abolition. Then the early church came swiftly to treat 'the sabbath' as a matter of indifference.

In the early days of the Jerusalem church one hears very little about 'the sabbath'. Christians soon came to realise that the death and resurrection of the Jesus had transformed the entire situation of the people of God. Gentile Christians were free to work out for themselves what day they wanted to meet on. They chose not to use the sabbath but to use the first day of the week. Paul taught that although the Mosaic law was holy, righteous and good, it was also temporary, and Christians were now released from it. The Spirit fulfils the law by walking in the Spirit. No New Testament letter ever hints that any kind of keeping of a holy day by Christians is obligatory. Galatians 4:10, Romans 14:5 and Colossians 2:16 are evidence that a Christian was free in these matters. Sunday was not a 'new sabbath'. It was simply useful to meet on one day a week and Sunday reminded the Christians of Jesus' resurrection and the outpouring of the Holy Spirit. But it was a matter of usefulness not legislation.

The old Saturday-sabbath of the Mosaic law is not fulfilled in a new 'holy day' at all! Sunday is a great and useful tradition in the Christian church. But this is a matter of Christian influence. It is wonderful when there is sufficient consensus about shops and businesses closing down for Sunday.

The sabbath spoke of 'entering into rest' as a spiritual experience. This is the heart of the matter for the Christian today.

In the original event of creation, 'sabbath' was a spiritual experience in the heart of God which men and women were able to share. God's activity in creation followed a threefold pattern. (i) The planning and the working was done by God. (ii) There came a point where the work was accomplished, and God rejoiced in what He had done. (iii) Men and women were to enter into the joy of what God had done.

This threefold pattern is the way in which God wants to work in His world. It is the way in which we are to live. (i) Life must be led and governed by God. (ii) Eventually God achieves His purpose. (iii) 'Entering into rest' is the occasion when we reap the benefits of what God has done. It is a large subject and cannot be explored in all of its fullness here. Entering into rest is the final consummation of God's covenant. It is when He swears the oath of the covenant and says – on oath – 'I will indeed bless you'.

Chapter 33

The Fifth and Sixth Commandments
(Exodus 20:12–13)

One might feel somewhat surprised that the command concerning parents is found at this point. It stands at the head of the fifth-to-ninth commands, in the same way that the first command stands at the head of the first-to-third. Like the other six of the first seven commands it is supported by the death penalty for disobedience. The reason for the eminence of **the fifth commandment** is that much more is involved than simply respect to parents. It was a command which held the entire nation together. It is noticeable that although national prosperity was promised to the nation if the law as a whole was obeyed, yet out of the ten commands it is the fifth that has the added phrase, *'in order that you may lengthen your days in the promised land . . . '*. This phrase could have been added to any of the ten commands yet it was added to the fifth. It is precisely this phrase that is quoted in the New Testament (Ephesians 6:1–4) – one of the rare places in the New Testament where one of the ten commands is explicitly cited. National stability is promised to Israel if this command is obeyed. The connection with the land is explicit.

In the system of land occupancy in ancient Israel (as envisaged by the Mosaic law) the family had extraordinary importance. Land tenure, military service, administration of the law, slavery, matters of marriage and divorce, all made use of the fact that the entire life of the nation was conducted through family units. Many of Israel's institutions, such as Levirate marriage, inheritance laws, the jubilee, were designed to protect the family. But of all the rulings that protected the family, the fifth commandment was the greatest. *'Give honour to your father*

115

and your mother in order that you may lengthen your days in the promised land that Yahweh your God is giving you' (20:12). To 'give honour' means to respect, to give precedence, to take a person seriously. It implies that parents would be respected. Their wishes would be valued. Their priority in authority would be accepted. Leviticus 19:3 demands that that they should be 'feared', that is, 'held in awe'.

The mother and father are equal in this respect. Although women were subordinate in authority in many ways, and the husband was the leader of the couple, yet in matters concerning the family she had co-authority with the husband and is to receive honour and respect with him.

Walking in the Spirit will lead to the fulfilment of the deepest intentions of the fifth commandment. The cultural overtones fall aside. In the last analysis the Christian is not 'under the law'. He is certainly not under the entire system of society into which the fifth commandment is interwoven. In Ephesians 5:18–21 Paul urges Christians to be 'filled with the Spirit' (Ephesians 5:18). His appeal to walk in the Spirit leads immediately to his instructions concerning husbands and wives (5:22–33), children and parents (6:1–4). In this context he quotes the fifth command, widening it in the phrase 'that you may live long on the earth'. The land of Israel has now become 'the earth' in Paul's revised version. Being filled with the Spirit will lead to the fulfilling of the law! Of all of the commands of the Mosaic law, this is one that requires little adaptation in the life of the Spirit. Jesus gave no hint that living under His resurrection would involve any retrograde step in this matter (see Mark 10:19), and it is almost the only piece of Mosaic legislation that Paul quotes without much emendation. However Paul adds remarks that are **not** in the law. Parents are not to provoke their children. That was not in the legislation from Moses! But walking in the Spirit would take care of that too. Elsewhere he urges respect for parents out of respect for Jesus (Colossians 3:20) but he does not mention that the law said the same.

The **sixth command** is one of the shortest: *'You shall not murder'*. The command obviously did not forbid capital punishment, since that was required in Israel in some situations. Equally it did not forbid the waging of war; certain situations in Israel led to war and this was not thought to be a breach of the sixth commandment. It did not forbid the killing of animals, since animal sacrifices were offered every day.

Life is created by God and is sacred. As early as Genesis 9:5–6 the taking of human life was generally forbidden and was itself to be punished by execution. It was an instruction given to the human race emerging in the line of Noah, long before it was part of the ten commandments. No 'ransoming' was allowed in this case. Toleration of the continued living of a murderer was regarded as defiling the land (Numbers 35:29–34). It is a biblical principle that punishment should be appropriate to the crime.

The Ten Commandments are modified in the 'leading of the Spirit' in at least four ways. Most of the ten commandments are included in 'the leading of the Spirit' without any lessening of the requirement. However there are at least four modifications. Firstly, the sabbath undergoes radical change and is not simplistically and literally kept by the Christian. Secondly, the **exposition** of the Ten Commandments contained in the rest of the law is **not** taken up in the leading of the Spirit. Thirdly, the penalties and sanctions are not mandatory. Christians do not apply punishment in precisely the same way that was applied in Israel. Fourthly, the ten commandments must be regarded as too **low** a standard for the individual Christian. Jesus transferred the governing authority over the Christian's life to Himself exclusively, and required (without expounding the law at all) an altogether higher way of living.

Chapter 34

The Seventh and Eighth Commandments
(Exodus 20:14–15)

The **seventh command**, originally, in ancient Israel, forbade a
sexual relationship between a man and a married woman within
the community of Israel. (Marriages with foreign women were
forbidden altogether – Deuteronomy 7:3–4.) Leviticus 18:20,
20:10, Numbers 5:11–15, Deuteronomy 5:18 and 22:22–24 refer
to the same crime. Leviticus 18:20 describes it as 'defilement' of
the land and includes in it a number of sexual offences. Any
who commit such things are to be cut off from among their
people' (Leviticus 18:29). 'Cutting off' in this verse seems to
refer to exclusion from Israel by means of execution. Both the
man and the woman are to be executed for such a crime by their
being stoned to death (Leviticus 20:10; Deuteronomy 22:22,
24). The law treated a betrothed woman as a married woman
for the purpose of this ruling (Deuteronomy 22:24). Adultery
was a crime requiring action by the community. It was not
simply a private matter.

A sexual relationship with a single girl was a different
crime (see Deuteronomy 22:28). The punishment for adultery
was death; the penalty for immorality with a single girl was
compulsory marriage without the possibility of divorce!

A sexual relationship with an unmarried slave-girl was taken
for granted as normal; she was a kind of second-class wife for
the slave-owner or his son. Judging from the story of Ruth
widows were in a similarly vulnerable position (see Ruth 2:8–9,
22; 3:10). Polygamy – having more than one wife – was not
against the Mosaic law. Nor was concubinage – having a female
slave who was sexually available, but who was not fully a wife.
Both the wife and the concubine had legal rights.

A concubine was not executed if she was found guilty of sexual liaison with a man other than her recognised partner. Her position was such that less loyalty was expected from her towards her husband (Leviticus 19:20). The guilty couple in this case were scourged.

Adultery was regarded as a very serious crime, so serious it was punished by death. It was worse than involvement with a prostitute (which the law did not forbid!) Much of this might surprise and horrify a Christian, but this is itself a reminder that the Mosaic law was considerably inferior to life in the Holy Spirit. The seventh commandment did not originally refer to everything that a modern Christian rightly considers to be immorality.

The wisdom literature went further than the law in insisting on a much fuller sexual purity. In Proverbs all marital infidelity is rebuked (Proverbs 5:1–23), yet still the adulteress is judged more severely than the harlot. 'A harlot seeks only for a loaf of bread, but another man's wife stalks a priceless soul' (Proverbs 6:26). Adultery is a devouring fire (Proverbs 6:20–35), and leads to ruin (Proverbs 7:1–27).

Why is adultery judged more severely than other similar sexual sins? Why does it attract the death penalty? The answer surely is that the Israelite law protected the family. Adultery was considered worse than other forms of immorality because it broke up another man's family. Adultery was placed on a level with murder; it has a murderous affect on the life of the family and therefore on the life of the nation. The family often owns property and cares for children. When the family-life of a nation is unstable the nation is unstable. The stability of Israel was important to God. He wanted the Israelites to 'live long in the land'. The death penalty for adultery protected the family in a powerful manner. The New Testament goes further than the Mosaic law in its requirement of sexual purity.

The **eighth command** brings us to the sanctity of property, the sanctity of private ownership. It says: *'You shall not steal'* (20:15; compare Deuteronomy 5:19). Whereas the command concerning adultery forbade theft of a man's wife, the command concerning stealing forbids theft of a man's property.

In ancient Israel the kinds of theft most mentioned are (i) the stealing of domestic animals (see Exodus 22:1–4), (ii) the forcible entry into a house or sheepfold (see Exodus 22:2–3), (iii) robbery (see Leviticus 5:21–26), There is no reason to agree with those who think that the command originally concerned kidnapping. 'Kidnapping' (unlike the kind of theft envisaged in the eighth command) was subject to the death penalty.

The breaking of the eighth commandment never involved the death penalty unless some other crime was also involved. In this respect Israel differed from surrounding nations in the ancient world. In other nations serious theft brought upon the criminal the death penalty. But in Israel, the punishment of theft involved restoration and compensation (see Exodus 22:1) or the thief might be sold as a slave (see Exodus 22:3). Theft was punished by the thief having to restore the property so that the person robbed was in the position he was in before. The theft of an animal was punished by the thief having to restore its value. In the case of an ox or sheep the value had to be given fourfold or fivefold (Exodus 22:1). If the animal was recovered the penalty was to pay double its value (Exodus 22:4). The money was not a fine paid to the state; it was compensation paid to the victim.

The thief was not to be executed, and sometimes the Old Testament even shows some sympathy for him. 'People do not despise a thief if he steals to satisfy his hunger when he is starving', says Proverbs 6:30. Yet even the starving thief is warned. 'Yet if he is caught, he must pay sevenfold, though it costs him all the wealth of his house' (Proverbs 6:31).

Penalties concerning theft did not involve mutilation (one thinks of Islamic law which in this matter is more severe). And it did not vary penalties according to the social status of the injured party, or of the criminal. The basic exhortation reappears in the gospel. The law condemns stealing; so does the gospel. There is an overlap of demand. The deepest requirements of the law are satisfied when the Christian obeys the Spirit.

'Do not take money by force' said John the Baptist to soldiers who asked his advice (Luke 3:14). 'You who preach against stealing, do you steal?' asked Paul (Romans 2:21), obviously regarding theft as plainly wicked. 'Teach slaves ... not to steal ... ', Paul said to Titus (Titus 2:10). 'Let none of you suffer as a thief', said Peter (1 Peter 4:15). Obviously the basic moral demand of the eighth commandment continues. Yet at no point do the apostolic writers after the Day of Pentecost specially draw attention to the eighth commandment. When condemning theft they do not say 'As Moses said ... ' or 'Do not steal and so keep the law of God'. That kind of specific placing of the Christian under the Mosaic law is something that they generally do not do. Ephesians 6:1–2 is virtually the only example and it is following up Ephesians 5:18! Life in the Spirit fulfils the law. The nearest the apostolic writers come to placing the Christian under the law is when – in certain areas covered by the Ten Commandments – they say virtually the same thing as the one of the Ten Commandments but apply it differently.

Chapter 35

The Ninth and Tenth Commandments
(Exodus 20:16–17)

The ninth commandment reads: *'You shall not bear false witness against your neighbour'* (Exodus 20:16). It is clear from the reference to 'testimony' that the command concerned giving accurate testimony in a law-court. It was not originally a general command about truth-telling. The Christian goes further than the Mosaic law. He or she will be led by the Spirit to live an open life and to live without the spirit of deceit. But we are not under any obligation to tell out everything we know to those who have no right to private information.

'Your neighbour' included anyone and everyone who might be brought before a court. Although the 'neighbour' would generally be someone within the community of Israel, yet the law also said 'The stranger who stays with you temporarily shall be to you on a level with the homeborn among you, and you shall love him as yourself' (Leviticus 19:34). In Exodus 11:2 'neighbour' refers to nearby Egyptians.

Jesus keeps the ninth commandment in the richest possible way. Jesus comes to the world and 'testifies' to it. When Jesus was on trial, His enemies produced false witnesses who twisted the facts concerning Jesus. But Jesus Himself, His self-testimony, His miracles and His Father's testimony to Him all present the straightforward truth concerning Jesus. Jesus Himself referred to the rules about legal testimony. 'In your law it is written that the testimony of two witnesses is valid. I am one who witnesses for myself; my other witness is the Father ...' (John 8:16–17).

The Christian is invited to be a 'witness' also. Jesus is the model for us. He gave faithful witness to Himself. Now we too are to stand before the world, conscious that Jesus is on trial, and we give our 'witness' concerning Jesus. The Christian is to be conscious that the 'courtroom' in which he presents his witness is the entire world. He is specially enabled by the Holy Spirit. 'You shall receive power when the Holy Spirit comes on you, and you will be my witnesses...' (Acts 1:8). The apostles were unique witnesses in that they literally witnessed the resurrection (see Acts 1:26) and boldly declared the facts of the case before the courtroom of the world. But even those who are not in a position to 'testify' to resurrection appearances may be witnesses by the Holy Spirit of the power of Jesus' kingdom at work in their lives. This is the greatest way of fulfilling the ninth commandment. A witness must testify (Leviticus 5:1). A truthful witness saves lives (Proverbs 14:25). Many Samaritans believed because of one woman's 'witness' (John 4:39); something similar may take place when we bear 'witness' to Jesus, as we know Him and have experienced Him. Like the apostles we – at our own level – are able to say 'We are witnesses and so is the Holy Spirit' (Acts 5:32). During His lifetime false witnesses came forward to speak against Him (Matthew 26:59–60); now He has ascended to heaven millions of witnesses are ready to step forward and speak in His favour.

The tenth commandment reads: *'You shall not covet your neighbour's house; you shall not covet you neighbour's wife, or his manservant, or his maidservant, or his ox, or his ass, or anything that is your neighbour's'* (Exodus 20:17).

The tenth commandment is of great importance and in some ways is entirely unique among the legislation of the Bible. The apostle Paul knew what he was talking about when he said 'I had not known covetousness if the law had not said "You shall not covet"' (Romans 7:7). It was this particular command that he chose when he made that remark. This is the law's most sharp and powerful command.

The tenth command internalises all of the other commands. It is only this command that can induce any kind of conviction of sin. This was Paul's point in Romans 7:7–25. In Romans 7:7–25 Paul takes up the question 'Is the law a sinful thing in itself?' His answer is 'No', but he says if we ever come under the command not to covet we shall discover that it gives an intense experience of what sin is like.

This introduces us to a vital point. There are two ways of taking the law of God. The law may be taken externally and it may be considered with special reference to 'covetousness'.

It was this command, and this command only that showed the law could be taken to refer to the heart after all. It was to be administered by magistrates, but there was this one line in it that could not be administered by magistrates. It showed that the real need of the people of Israel was for a heart that did not even want to sin.

The tenth command defines the need of the human race. The problem with the human race is that we are all born with our desires and appetites out of control. Out of the heart – said Jesus – come various kinds of 'covetings' (Mark 7:22). What really matters is the heart. Sin does not consist in religious ceremony or lack of religious ceremony. Sin does not consist merely in failure of intellectual understanding. Sin and righteousness consist of what is taking place in the heart. The trouble with men and women is that we are born with sin in the 'heart' – the central core of the human personality. Out of the heart come many inclinations to sin and malice and impurity (Mark 7:20–22). These arise within a man or woman's life. It is not failure to wash the hand that 'defiles' man, as was thought by the Pharisees of Mark 7. Nor is it a failure in education or intellect, as tends to be thought by modern people. The fountainhead of all human problems – ultimately – is failure to control the wickedness within. Each person is tempted when he is enticed by his own desires (James 1:14).

Chapter 36

Restraint By Fear

(Exodus 20:18–26)

In Exodus 20:18–21 the story now tells us what was happening as the law was being given.

1. **The law restrains by fear**. Awe-inspiring phenomena were continuing to be seen and heard as the law was being announced by God (20:18).

2. **The law creates distance between God and His people**. There was nothing encouraging for the people as the law was being given. The law did not bring them near to God; it drove them away. They said to Moses, *'You speak with us, and we shall listen, but do not let God speak to us, lest we die'* (20:19). Another result of the giving of the law is that the people dislike close contact with God.

3. **The law is given 'on account of transgressions'**. Moses explains the situation. God has tested the people before, but now the fearful phenomena on Mount Sinai is a further testing from God. Exodus 20:20 is a key statement and gives us a vital commentary on the purpose of the law. It is surely the explanation of Paul's remark that the law was given 'on account of sin' (Galatians 3:19).

Its background is to be seen in the various occasions when God had tested Israel and they had failed the test. Before they have been sinfully unwilling to listen to Moses, and unwilling to trust in God at a time of testing. Now they will do anything. 'We shall listen to you!', they say. What has made the difference is that now they are afraid to disobey. The law is producing a measure of obedience in them; it is the result of fear of God's glory.

Moses explains what has happened. God has come so that the fear of Him may be upon the people to keep them from sinning. This was precisely Paul's point in Galatians 3:19.

Exodus 20:21 brings this little unit to a close. *'And the people stood at a distance, and Moses approached the thick darkness where God was'.* Now further details of the requirements of the law must be given. Moses ascends the mountain yet again.

The law of Moses is not the way in which Christian obedience is produced. 'For you have not come to what may be touched', says the epistle to the Hebrews referring to this very passage, '. . . to a blazing fire, and darkness, and gloom and a tempest, and the sound of a trumpet, and a voice whose words made the hearers entreat that no further messages be spoken to them . . .' (Hebrews 12:18–19). 'You have not come to that!' says the New Testament. There could scarcely be a stronger statement that the method of producing 'holiness' is quite different from what was operating at Sinai.

Moses draws near to the thick darkness (20:21). He hears a voice but he is not allowed to see the glory of God on Sinai. God speaks and is given a message to pass on to the Israelites (20:22). They have had the experience of literally hearing God speak to them in an audible voice. The entire people, including Moses, had stood at the foot of the mountain and had heard God speak to them. Now the people want this privilege no longer. They are afraid. The rest of the law given at this time will come through the mediation of Moses. Exodus 20:22– 23:19 will all be sheer legislation. This section of Exodus, chapters 20:22–23:33, is called 'the book of the covenant' (see 24:7). First comes a short prologue (20:22–26) and then the regulations begin with the words in Exodus 21:1, *'These are the "cases"'* (or 'decisions' – *mishpatim*).

Moses had been with the people while the Ten Command- ments were given. The rest of the law is given to Moses alone who must hand on to the people what God has said to him (20:22–23:33). All of 20:22–23:33 is given to Moses on the lower slopes of Sinai. The people withdrew from hearing God audibly on the lower part of the mountain (see 20:18–21). After the law of 20:23–23:33 has been given to Moses he will ascend to the top of the mountain.

God had spoken to the people without making any use of images. They had heard His voice (20:22) but no visible model of any god was used, neither should there be in the future any representations of God (20:23). *'Do not make any gods to be alongside me; you are not to make for yourself gods of silver and gods of gold'* (20:23). It seems this is the central emphasis at this point. Two of the ten commandments are being reinforced and developed, the first (Exodus 20:3) and the second (Exodus 20:4–6). They must not have another god besides Yahweh, and they must not make an idol, a physical representation of God.

Another word of command concerns how the Israelites will make an altar. The altar must be made of earth. It must not be made of stone (20:24–25) and must be simple in design. There must be no stairs at the side of the altar; the absence of stairs will prevent immodesty (20:26). Other nations had priests who wore short aprons but otherwise were almost naked. Israel's law demanded longer outer garments; it forbade steps up to the top of the altar; and it demanded the priest wear underclothing (see Exodus 28:42).

The Christian has very little to do with this kind of regulation; he does not need it directly. Yet it reminds each Christian that he too is a 'priest' in a sense. He does not work in an earthly temple in Jerusalem, but he has a priestly ministry to the people around him. He intercedes for them. He advises them and counsels them, pointing to the God of the Bible who wants to be reconciled to them. He presents to people around him the sacrifice of Jesus upon the cross. His modesty will come through his following the leading of the Holy Spirit. It is the kind of area where we are to trust the Holy Spirit and follow obvious principles of wisdom and love towards others. Like the healed demoniac (Mark 5:15; Luke 8:35), anyone who is led by the Holy Spirit will be 'clothed and in his right mind'! The fact that this prologue to the 'Book of the Covenant' is specially concerned with idolatry and corrupt worship lets us know that the foundations of any relationship with God is to be found in realisation of who God is, and true worship of Him. God

Himself is the foundation of every aspect of the life of His people. If the people have the slightest tendency to idolatry or debased worship, their entire status as the people of God will be threatened. Some sins are more destructive than others. Idolatry and perverted worship is the most fatal dishonour to God, and will entirely destroy the reality of their being the people of God.

Idolatry was supremely the fatal crime – and still is. The people of God could survive despite times of great weakness, but they could not survive times of idolatry. We may learn from this that of all the outrages that God hates, the greatest takes place when He Himself is misrepresented.